B♭ EDITION

THE HAL LEONARD

REAL JAZZ BOOK

OVER 500 SONGS

HAL LEONARD REAL JAZZ BOOK

ISBN 0-7935-9106-6

HAL•LEONARD®
CORPORATION

7777 W. BLUEMOUND RD. P.O. BOX 13819 MILWAUKEE, WI 53213

Visit Hal Leonard Online at
www.halleonard.com

THE HAL LEONARD
REAL JAZZ BOOK

CONTENTS

COMPOSER/LYRICIST INDEX

ADIOS

English Words by EDDIE WOODS
Spanish Translation and Music by ENRIC MADRIGUERA

AFTER ALL

By MIKE STERN

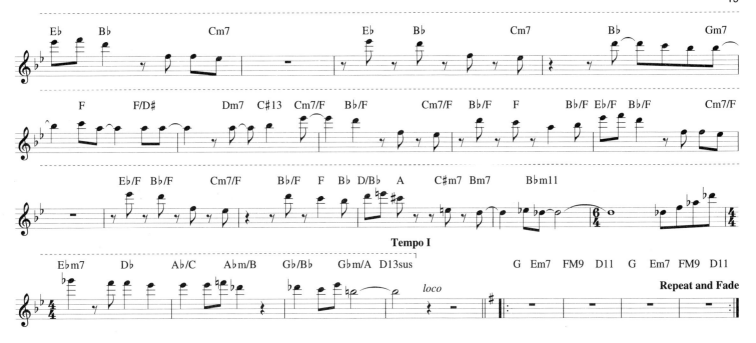

AFFIRMATION

By JOSE FELICIANO

ÁGUAS DE MARÇO
(Waters of March)

Words and Music by
ANTONIO CARLOS JOBIM

AFTER THE RAIN

By JOHN COLTRANE

ÁGUA DE BEBER
(Water to Drink)

Original Words by VINICIUS DE MORAES
English Words by NORMAN GIMBEL
Music by ANTONIO CARLOS JOBIM

AFTERMATH (PART II)

Written by KEVIN EUBANKS

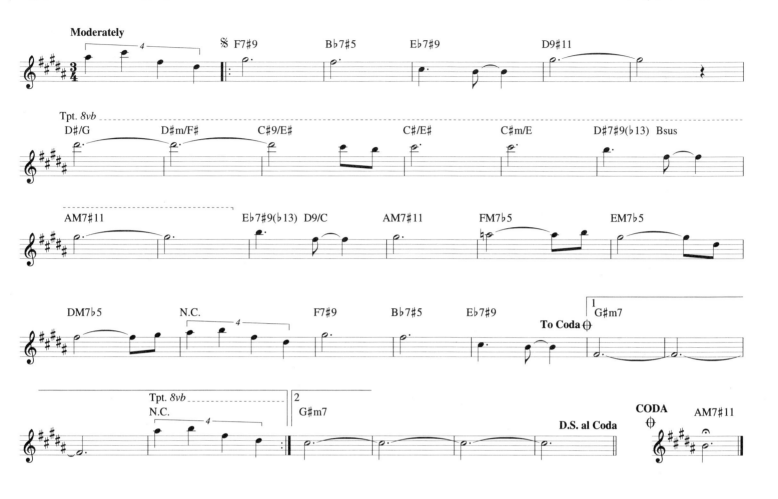

AIN'T SHE SWEET

Words by JACK YELLEN
Music by MILTON AGER

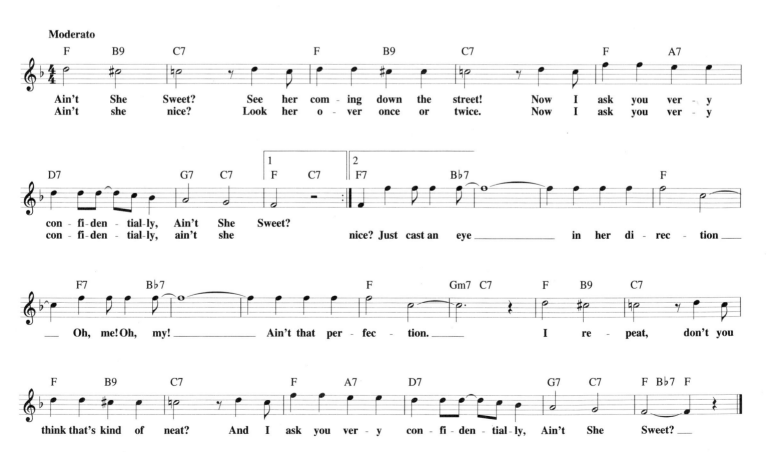

24

AIR DANCING

© 1987 Buster Williams Productions, Inc. (SESAC)
All Rights Administered by Soroka Music Ltd.

By BUSTER WILLIAMS

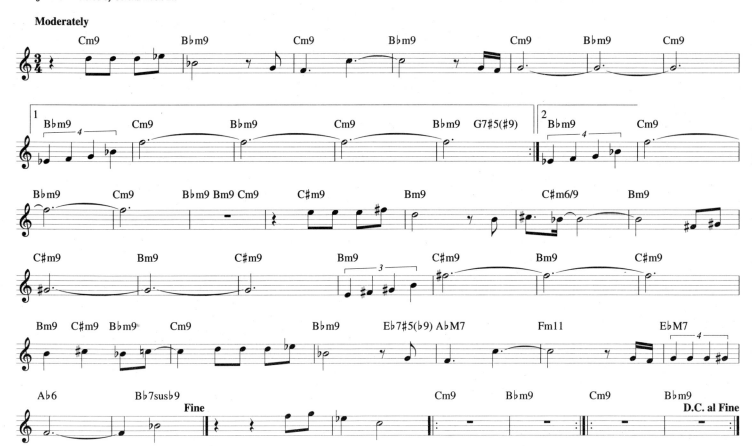

AISHA

Copyright © 1962 Aisha Music Company
Copyright Renewed

By McCOY TYNER

AJA

Words and Music by WALTER BECKER
and DONALD FAGEN

Additional Lyrics

2. Upon the hill they've got time to burn.
There's no return
Double Helix in the sky tonight.
Throw out the hardware
Let's do it right.

3. Upon the hill they think I'm okay.
Okay so they say.
Chinese music always sets me free.
Angular banjoes sound good to me.

ALABAMA

By JOHN COLTRANE

ALFIE
Theme from the Paramount Picture ALFIE

Words by HAL DAVID
Music by BURT BACHARACH

ALICE IN WONDERLAND
from Walt Disney's ALICE IN WONDERLAND

Words by BOB HILLIARD
Music by SAMMY FAIN

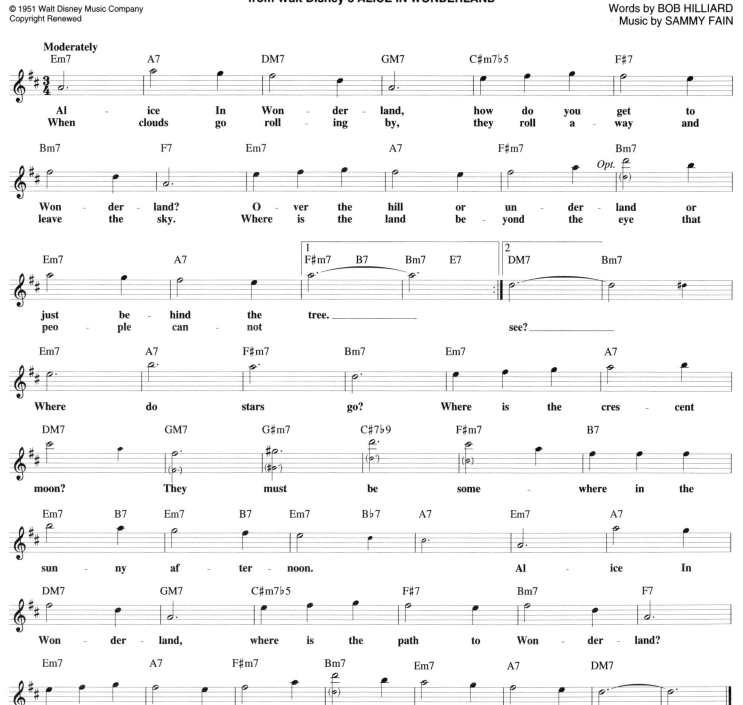

ALL ALONE

Words and Music by
IRVING BERLIN

ALONE TOO LONG
from BY THE BEAUTIFUL SEA

Words by DOROTHY FIELDS
Music by ARTHUR SCHWARTZ

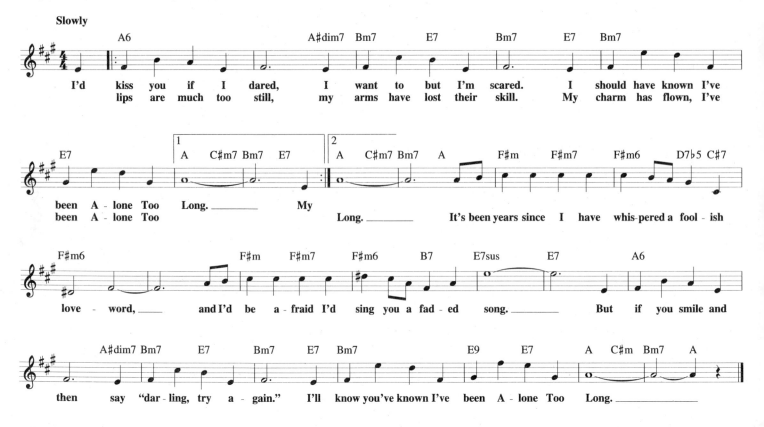

AND I THINK ABOUT IT ALL THE TIME

By ERNIE WATTS
and RAY DEWEY

30

ANTHROPOLOGY

By CHARLIE PARKER
and DIZZY GILLESPIE

ANTIGUA

By ANTONIO CARLOS JOBIM

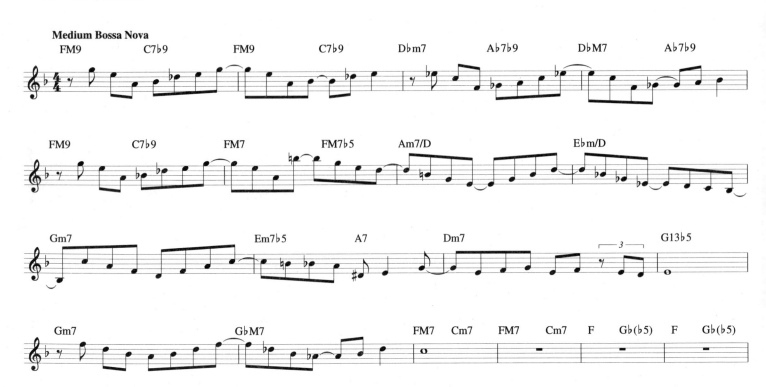

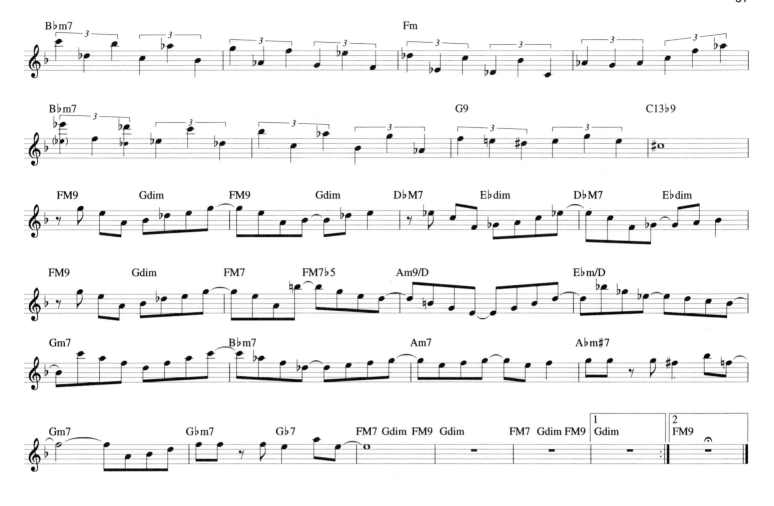

APRIL IN PARIS

Words by E.Y. HARBURG
Music by VERNON DUKE

ARE YOU HAVIN' ANY FUN?
from GEORGE WHITE'S SCANDALS (1939 Edition)

Words by JACK YELLEN
Music by SAMMY FAIN

ARMANDO'S RHUMBA

By CHICK COREA

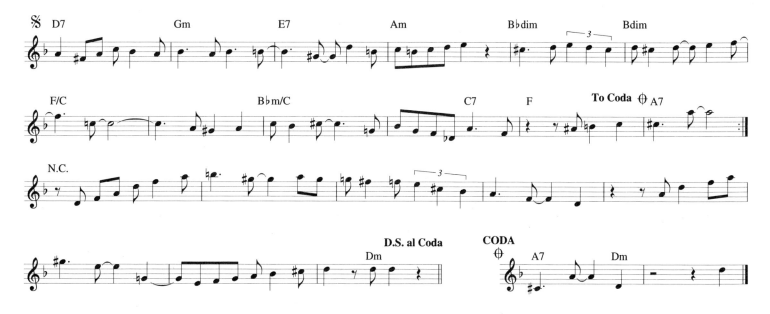

AS LONG AS I LIVE

Lyric by TED KOEHLER
Music by HAROLD ARLEN

AT LONG LAST LOVE
from YOU NEVER KNOW

Words and Music by
COLE PORTER

ASHES TO ASHES

Music by JOE SAMPLE

AUNT HAGAR'S BLUES

Words by J. TIM BRYMN
Music by W.C. HANDY

AUTUMN IN NEW YORK

Words and Music by
VERNON DUKE

BARK FOR BARKSDALE

By GERRY MULLIGAN

BAJA BAJO

By JOHN PATITUCCI
and CHICK COREA

BASS DESIRES

By PETER ERSKINE

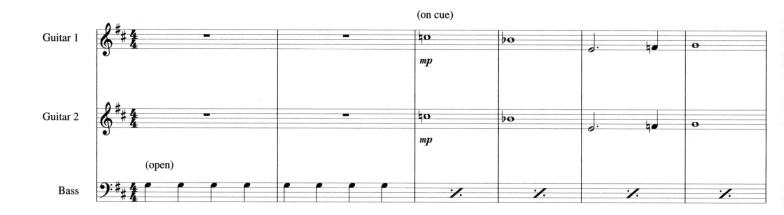

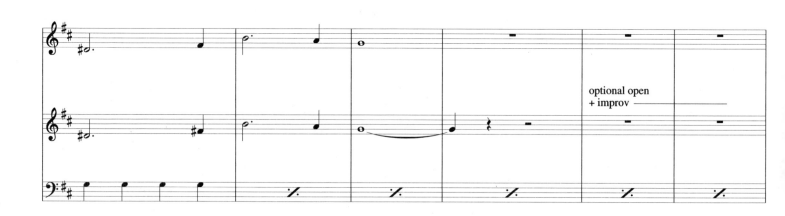

to improvisation
"time, no changes"...

BEAUTIFUL LOVE

Words by HAVEN GILLESPIE
Music by VICTOR YOUNG, WAYNE KING
and EGBERT VAN ALSTYNE

BEFORE YOU GO

By MIKE STERN

BÉSAME MUCHO
(Kiss Me Much)

Original Words and Music by CONSUELO VELAZQUEZ
English Words by SUNNY SKYLAR

BESSIE'S BLUES

By JOHN COLTRANE

Bright Blues

THE BEST THING FOR YOU
from the Stage Production CALL ME MADAM

Words and Music by
IRVING BERLIN

Moderately

BETTER LUCK NEXT TIME
from the Motion Picture Irving Berlin's EASTER PARADE

Words and Music by
IRVING BERLIN

Freely

G/B B♭dim7 Am7 D7 Am7 D7♭9 GM7 B/D♯ Ddim7

For ev - 'ry rose that with - ers and dies, an - oth - er blooms in its stead. A new love waits to

C♯m7 F♯7 C♯m7 F♯7♭9 BM7 Am7 D7 Bm7 E7♭9

o - pen its eyes af - ter the old love is dead. That sounds all right in a care - less rhyme,

Am7 D7 F7♯11 E7♭9 **Moderately** Am7 D7 G G♯dim7 D7/A B7♯5

but there's sel - dom a sec - ond time. Bet - ter Luck Next Time, that could nev - er be, ___ be - cause there

CM7 C♯dim7 D7 D7♭9 G6 Em7 Am7 D7♯5(♭9) Am7 D7

ain't gon - na be no next time for me, no sir - ee. ___ Made up my mind to make an - oth - er

G G♯dim7 D7/A B7♯5 CM7 C♯dim7 D7 D7♭9 G6 Am9 D7♭9 G6

start, ___ I've made my mind up, but I can't make up my heart. ___ I'd like a

F♯m9 B7 B7♯5 ³ DM7/E E9 C♯7/G♯ D/A Bm7 ³ Em7 A7

new luck - y day ___ that would be nice, ___ but this comes just once in a life - time, not

Am7/D D7 Am7 A7 D7 Cdim7 Bm7♭5 E7♭9

twice. ___ So don't say "Bet - ter Luck Next Time." That could nev - er be, ___ be - cause there

Am7 Cm♯7 G/D D9 | 1. G6 Em9 Am9 D7♯5(♭9) | 2. G6 Cm G6/9

ain't gon - na be no next time for me. ___ me. ___

BIG NICK

By JOHN COLTRANE

Moderately slow

AM7 F♯m7 Bm7 E7 AM7 F♯m7 Bm7 E7

A A7/C♯ D D♯dim A/E F♯7 Bm7 E7

AM7 F♯m7 Bm7 E7 AM7 F♯m7 Bm7 E7 A A7/C♯

D D♯dim A/E F♯7 Bm7 E7 A

BETWEEN THE DEVIL AND THE DEEP BLUE SEA
from RHYTHMANIA

Lyric by TED KOEHLER
Music by HAROLD ARLEN

BIJOU

Music by RALPH BURNS

BILL
from SHOW BOAT

Lyrics by P.G. WODEHOUSE and OSCAR HAMMERSTEIN II
Music by JEROME KERN

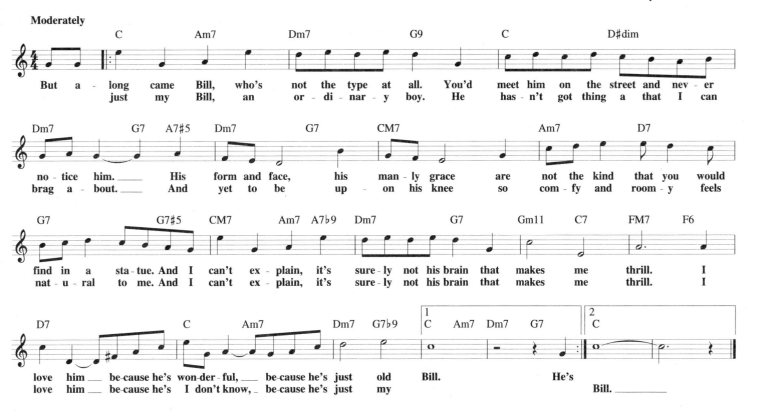

A BLOSSOM FELL

Words and Music by HOWARD BARNES,
HAROLD CORNELIUS and DOMINIC JOHN

BIRK'S WORKS

Music by JOHN "DIZZY" GILLESPIE

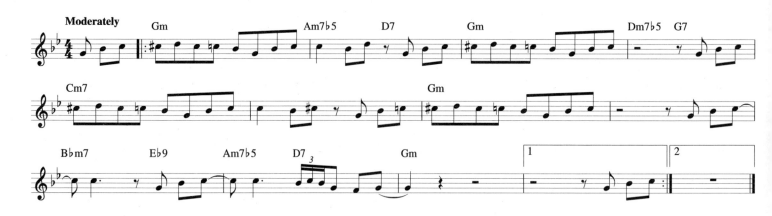

(What Did I Do to Be So)
BLACK AND BLUE
from AIN'T MISBEHAVIN'

Words by ANDY RAZAF
Music by HARRY BROOKS and FATS WALLER

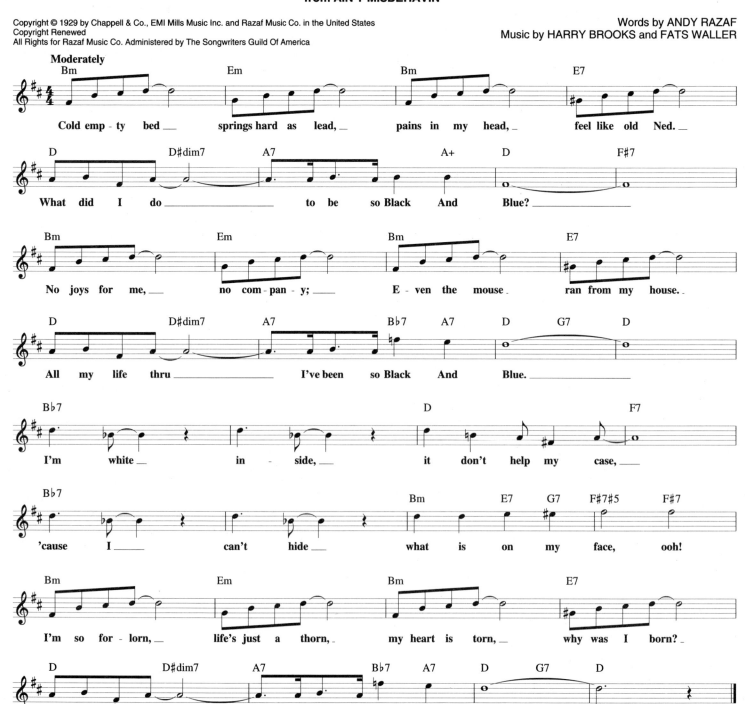

BLACK AND TAN FANTASY

By DUKE ELLINGTON
and BUB MILEY

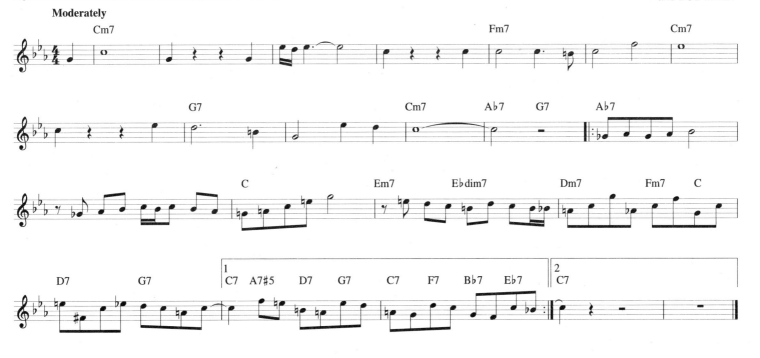

BLUE FLAME

Lyric by LEO CORDAY
Music by JAMES NOBLE and JOE BISHOP

BLACK COFFEE

Words and Music by PAUL FRANCIS WEBSTER
and SONNY BURKE

Feel - in' low as the ground. It's driv-in' me cra-zy, this wait-in' for my ba - by,
Feel - in' low as can be, It's driv-in' me cra-zy, this wait-in' for my ba - by,

to may - be come a - round. I'm
to may - be come a - round.

BLACK ORPHEUS

Words and Music by
LUIZ BONFÁ

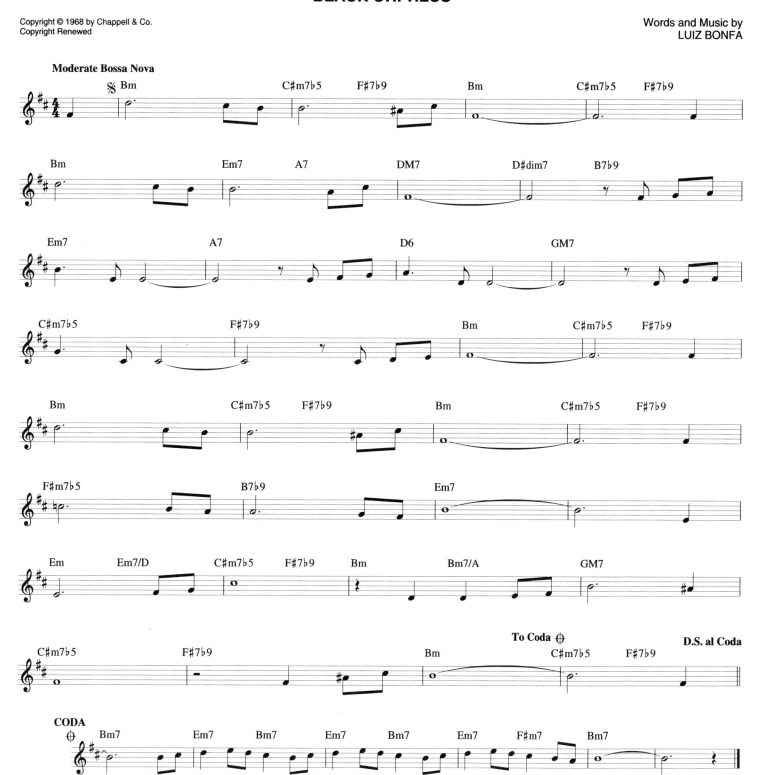

BLACK MARKET

Music by JOSEF ZAWINUL

Repeat ad lib.

BLACKBERRY WINTER

Words and Music by ALEC WILDER
and LOONIS McGLOHON

BLAME IT ON MY YOUTH

Words by EDWARD HEYMAN
Music by OSCAR LEVANT

BLUE TRAIN
(Blue Trane)

By JOHN COLTRANE

BLUE PRELUDE

Words by GORDON JENKINS
Music by JOE BISHOP

Slow Blues

Let me sigh, let me cry when I'm blue. Let me go 'way from this
lone - ly town. _____ Won't be long till my song will be thru', _____ 'cause I
know I'm on my last _____ go - round. _____ All the love I could steal, beg or bor - row _____
_____ would-n't heal all this pain in my soul. _____ What is love, but a pre - lude to
sor - row _____ with a heart - break a - head for your goal. _____ Here I go, now you
know why I'm leav - ing; _____ Got the blues, what can I lose, _____ good - bye. _____

BLUE STAR

Words by EDWARD HEYMAN
Music by VICTOR YOUNG

Slowly

Blue Star _____ when I am blue, all I do _____ is look at you. For
I seem to find peace of mind, and I nev - er get lone - ly when you
shine from a - far. _____ With you _____ a - way up there, I don't
dare _____ to have a care. For I want to show that your glow let's me
know that you know that I'm not blue. Blue Star. _____ Blue Star. _____

THE BLUE ROOM
from THE GIRL FRIEND

Words by LORENZ HART
Music by RICHARD RODGERS

BLUES FOR ALICE

By CHARLIE PARKER

BLUEPORT

By ART FARMER

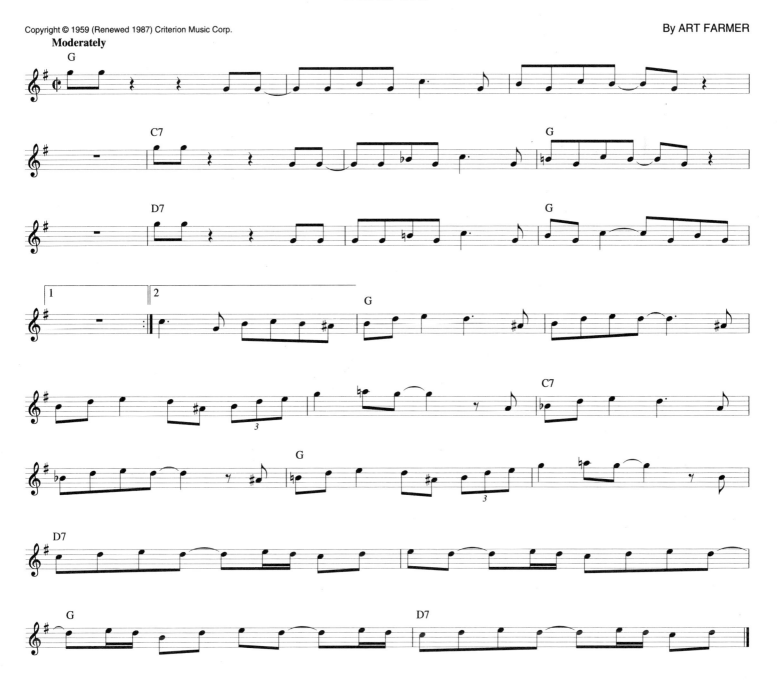

BLUES IN TIME

By PAUL DESMOND

BLUES FOR D.P.

Written by RON CARTER

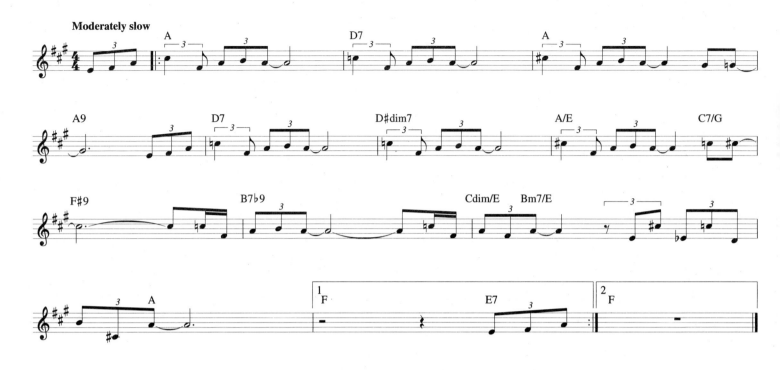

BLUES MARCH

By BENNY GOLSON

BLUES FOR JUNIOR
(Pyramid)

By RAY BROWN

BOSSA ANTIGUA

By PAUL DESMOND

BLUES FOR ROSALINDA

By FRANK MORGAN

BROADWAY

Words and Music by BILL BYRD,
TEDDY McRAE and HENRI WOODE

BORN TO BE BAD

Music by JOE SAMPLE

BOTH SIDES OF THE COIN

By MICHAEL BRECKER

BRAZIL

Words and Music by S.K. RUSSELL
and ARY BARROSO

BREAKIN' AWAY

Words and Music by AL JARREAU,
JAY GRAYDON and TOM CANNING

Just Break-in' A - way, ___ your love ___ has o - pened eyes that could - n't see. ___

Break-in' A - way, ___ your bea - con in ___ the night ___

___ dis - cov - ered me ___ Break - in' A - way, ___

BLUES ON TIME

Copyright © by Toots Music

By JEAN "TOOTS" THIELEMANS

Slow Blues

BLUISH GREY

Copyright © 1987 Jazz Editions

Composed by THAD JONES

Moderately slow

BOOZE BROTHERS

Composed by FRANK FOSTER

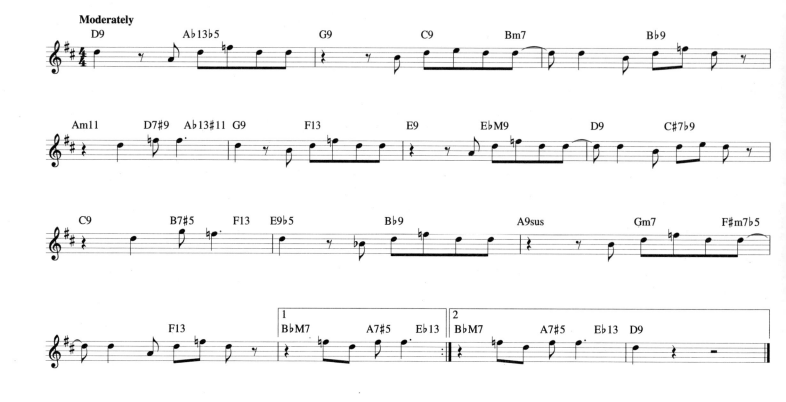

BUSTER'S LAST STAND

Written by GIL EVANS
and CLAUDE THORNHILL

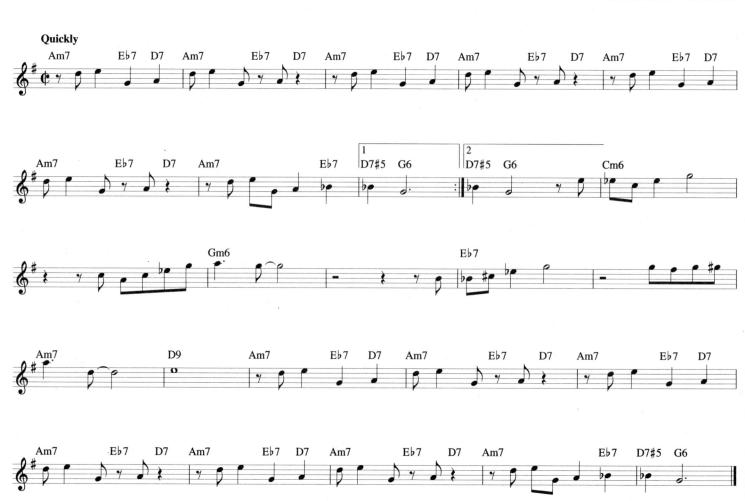

BULLET TRAIN

By LEE RITENOUR
and ERNIE WATTS

BYRD LIKE

By FREDDIE HUBBARD

CALL ME IRRESPONSIBLE
from the Paramount Picture PAPA'S DELICATE CONDITION

Words by SAMMY CAHN
Music by JAMES VAN HEUSEN

Can't Take You Nowhere

Music by TINY KAHN and AL COHEN
Words by DAVE FRISHBERG

CAPTAIN FINGERS

By LEE RITENOUR

CANTELOPE ISLAND

By HERBIE HANCOCK

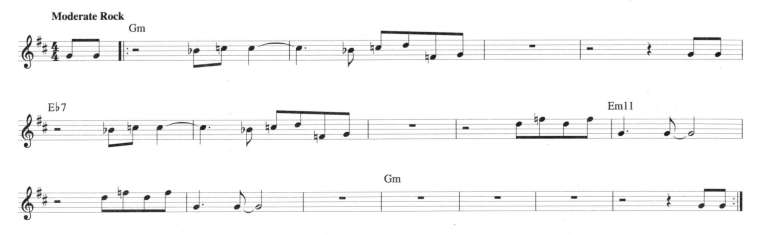

CATCHING THE SUN

By JAY BECKENSTEIN

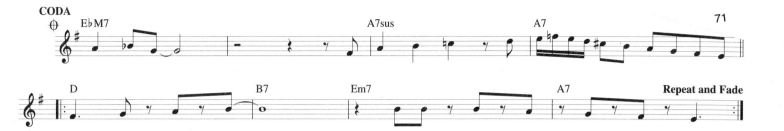

CAKE WALKING BABIES FROM HOME

Words and Music by HENRY TROY,
CHRIS SMITH and CLARENCE WILLIAMS

CAREFUL

By JAMES S. HALL

CANNONBALL

Music by JOSEF ZAWINUL

CARAVAN
from SOPHISTICATED LADIES

Words and Music by DUKE ELLINGTON,
IRVING MILLS and JUAN TIZOL

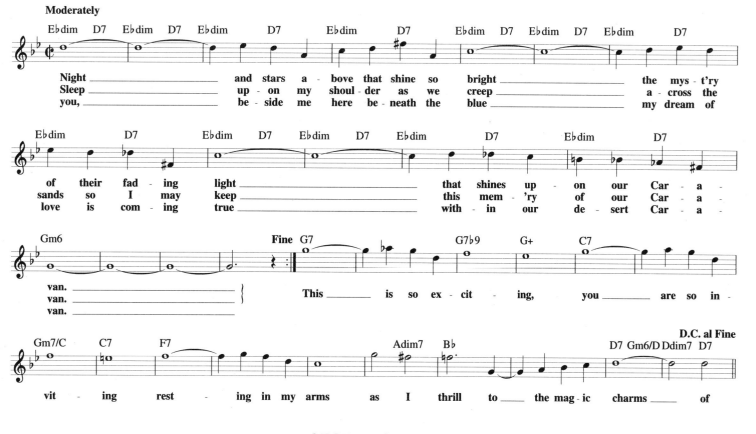

CECILIA IS LOVE

Composed by FRANK FOSTER

CAROLINA SHOUT

By JAMES P. JOHNSON

75

CAST YOUR FATE TO THE WIND

Words and Music by VINCE GUARALDI
and CAREL WERVER

CHAMELEON

By HERBIE HANCOCK, PAUL JACKSON,
HARVEY MASON and BENNIE MAUPIN

CHANGE PARTNERS
from the RKO Radio Motion Picture CAREFREE

Words and Music by
IRVING BERLIN

C'EST SI BON
(It's So Good)

English Words by JERRY SEELEN
French Words by ANDRE HORNEZ
Music by HENRI BETTI

CHRISTINA

By BUSTER WILLIAMS

CHANGE OF SEASON

By JOHN PATITUCCI

CHASIN' THE TRANE

By JOHN COLTRANE

A CHILD IS BORN

By THAD JONES

COCKTAILS FOR TWO
from the Paramount Picture MURDER AT THE VANITIES

Words and Music by ARTHUR JOHNSTON
and SAM COSLOW

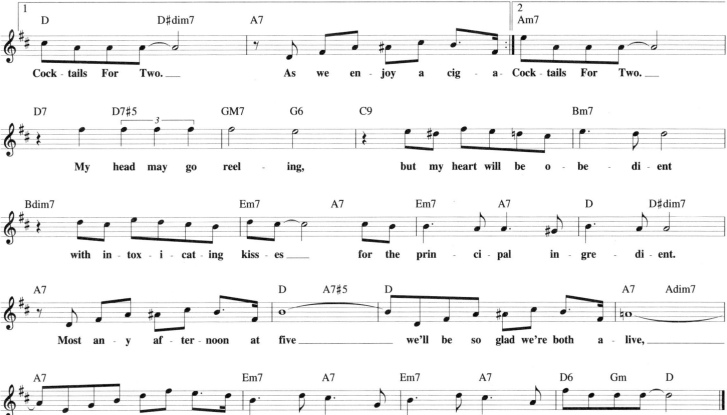

CHROMOZONE

By MIKE STERN

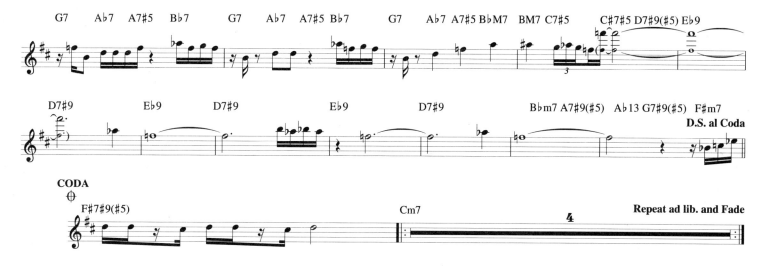

COME BACK TO ME
from ON A CLEAR DAY YOU CAN SEE FOREVER

Lyrics by ALAN JAY LERNER
Music by BURTON LANE

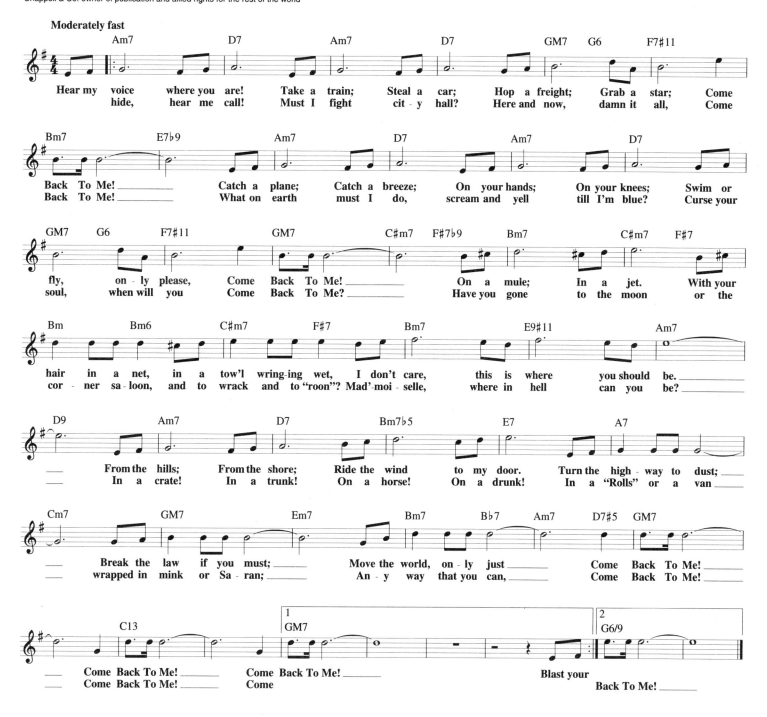

CON ALMA

Music by JOHN "DIZZY" GILLESPIE

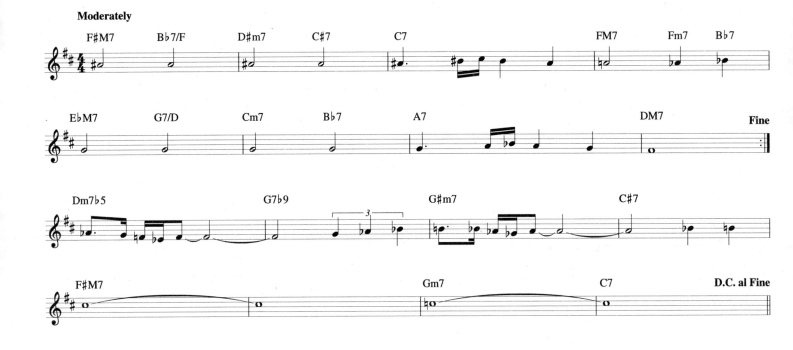

CONCEPTION

By GEORGE SHEARING

CONTINENTAL BLUES

By ERNIE WATTS

COUSIN MARY

By JOHN COLTRANE

THE CRAVE

By FERDINAND "JELLY ROLL" MORTON

DAHOMEY DANCE

By JOHN COLTRANE

COPENHAGEN

Lyric by WALTER MELROSE
Music by CHARLIE DAVIS

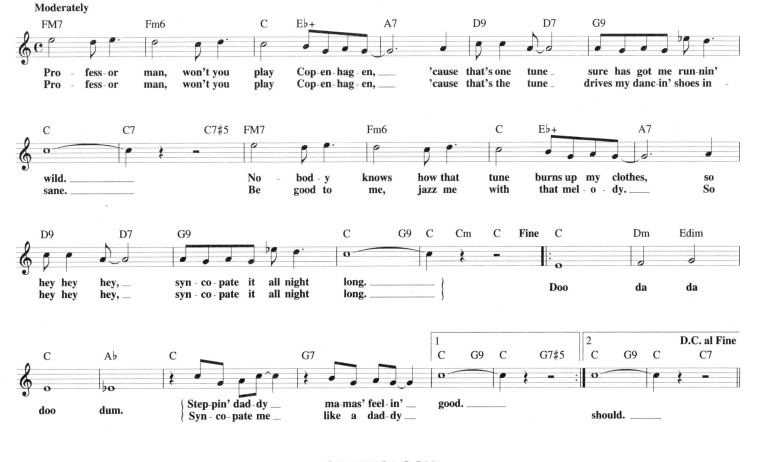

CRAZYOLOGY

By BENNIE HARRIS

THE CREOLE LOVE CALL

By DUKE ELLINGTON

THE DAWN OF TIME

Written by JOE LOVANO

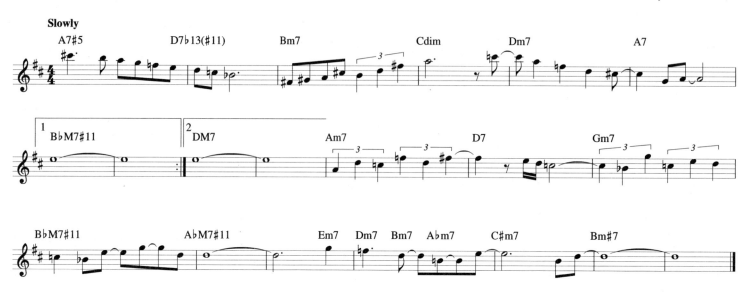

DANCING ON THE CEILING
from SIMPLE SIMON

Words by LORENZ HART
Music by RICHARD RODGERS

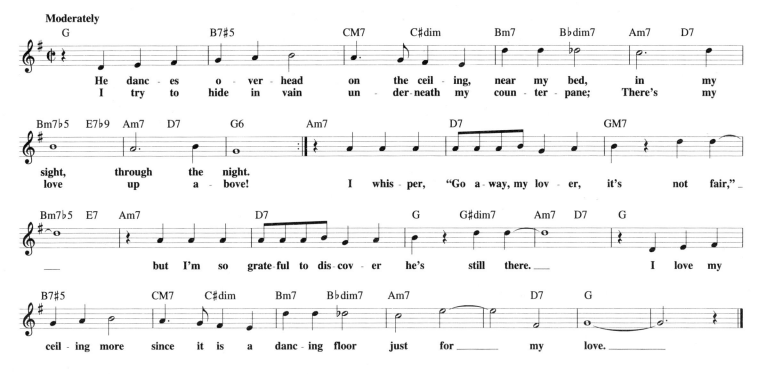

DARLING, JE VOUS AIME BEAUCOUP
from LOVE AND HISSES

Words and Music by
ANNA SOSENKO

CROSS MY HEART

By LEE RITENOUR
and ERIC TAGG

B/C#
___ no one in this world could make ___ me want to.

AM7 ... B/C# ... CM7
Put my love in-to jeo-par-dy, ___ noth-in' in this world could

Am7 ... C/D ... Gm7 ... Bb ... C6
take my heart a-way. ___

Gm7 Bb C6 Am7 Gm7 Bb C6 Am7

Bb C(add2) Dsus2 Gm7 Bb C6
Cross My Heart.

Gm7 Bb C6 Am7 Gm7 Bb C6 Am7
Cross My Heart, ___ I would

Bb C(add2) Dsus2 Gm7 Bb
nev-er tell ___ you ___ lies. ___ Cross My Heart, ___

C6 Gm7 Bb C6 Am7 Gm7 Bb
try to be-lieve ___ me. So Cross My Heart, ___

C6 Am Bb C(add2) Dsus2 Repeat and Fade
I would nev-er tell ___ you ___ lies. ___ Cross My Heart,

DECEPTACON

By BUSTER WILLIAMS

Moderately

A7sus ... F#m7b5

C7#9 ... Dsus

Ab7#9/Bb Eb7#9/F# ... FM7b5 ... EbM7#11 DbM7 EbM7#11

DOCTOR JAZZ
from JELLY'S LAST JAM

Lyric by WALTER MELROSE
Music by JOSEPH "KING" OLIVER

Oh, Hel-lo Cen-tral, give me Doc-tor Jazz, _____ he's got just what I need, I'll say he has. _____ When the world goes wrong, _____ and I _____ got the blues, he's _____ the man who makes me get out both my danc-ing shoes. _____ The more I get, the more I want, it seems. _____ I page old Doc-tor Jazz _ in all my dreams. _____ When I'm trou-ble bound and mixed, _ he's the guy that gets me fixed. _ Hel-lo, Central, give me Doc-tor Jazz. _____

CRYSTAL SILENCE

Music by CHICK COREA

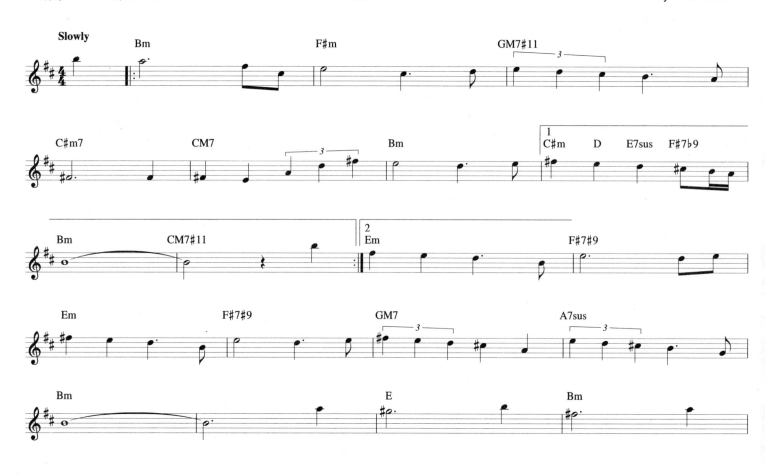

CUPCAKE

By BENNY GREEN

DAT DERE

Music by BOBBY TIMMONS
Lyrics by OSCAR BROWN, JR.

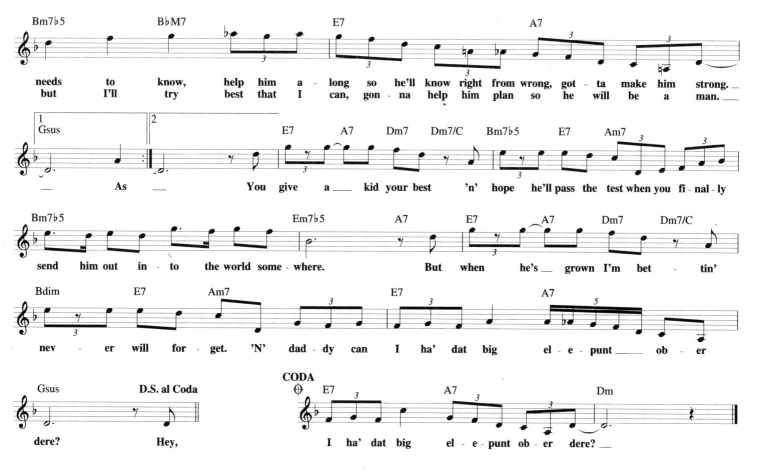

needs to know, help him a long so he'll know right from wrong, got ta make him strong.
but I'll try best that I can, gon na help him plan so he will be a man. ___

1 ___ As ___

2 ___ You give a ___ kid your best 'n' hope he'll pass the test when you fi nal ly

send him out in to the world some - where. But when he's ___ grown I'm bet - tin'

nev - er will for - get. 'N' dad - dy can I ha' dat big el - e - punt ___ ob - er

dere? Hey,

CODA I ha' dat big el - e - punt ob - er dere? ___

DON'T WORRY 'BOUT ME
from COTTON CLUB PARADE

Lyric by TED KOEHLER
Music by RUBE BLOOM

Moderately

Don't Wor - ry 'Bout Me, ___ I'll get a - long; ___ For - get a - bout me, ___

___ be hap - py, my love. ___ Let's say that our lit - tle show is o - ver and so, the sto - ry ends; ___

___ Why not call it a day the sen - si - ble way, and still be friends. ___ "Look

out for your - self" ___ should be the rule; ___ Give your heart and your love to whom -

ev - er you love, don't be a fool. ___ Dar - ling, why should you cling to some fad - ing thing that

used to be? ___ If you can for - get, Don't Wor - ry 'Bout Me. ___

DON'T YOU KNOW I CARE
(Or Don't You Care to Know)

Words by MACK DAVID
Music by DUKE ELLINGTON

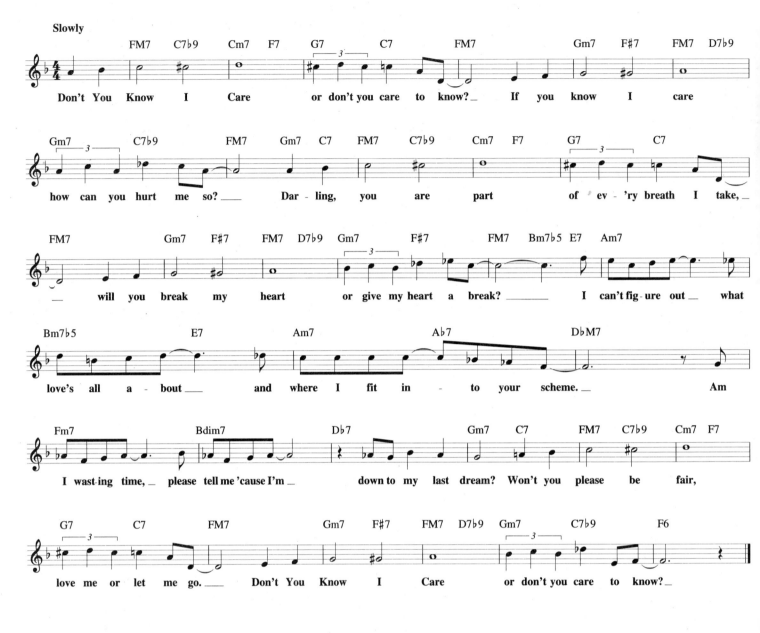

CURVES AHEAD

By RUSS FREEMAN

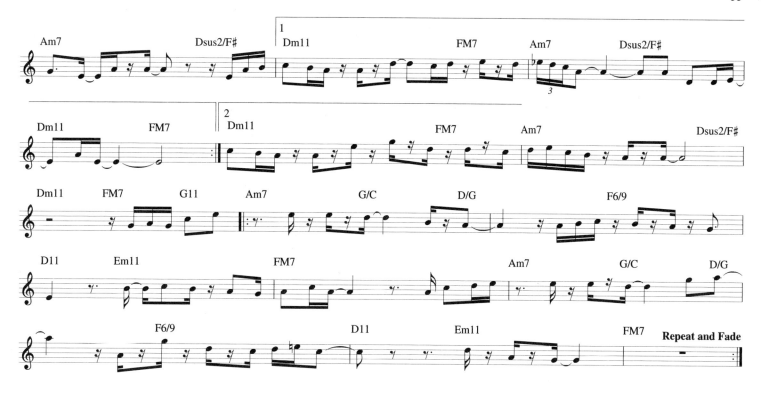

DREAM A LITTLE DREAM OF ME

TRO - © Copyright 1930 (Renewed) and 1931 (Renewed) Essex Music, Inc., Words and Music, Inc., New York, NY, Don Swan Publications, Miami, FL and Gilbert Keyes Music, Hollywood, CA

Words by GUS KAHN
Music by WILBUR SCHWANDT
and FABIAN ANDREE

DETOUR AHEAD

By HERB ELLIS,
JOHN FRIGO and LOU CARTER

DIMINUSHING

By DJANGO REINHARDT

DON'T SMOKE IN BED

By WILLIARD ROBINSON

Slowly

She left a note on her dress - er and her old wed-ding ring. With these few good - bye words,

sad - ly she sings: Good-bye old sleep-y head, __ I'm pack-ing you in. __ Like I said, __ take care of

ev-'ry-thing. __ I'm leav-ing my wed-ding ring. __ Don't look for me, __ I'll get a - head. __

Re - mem - ber, dar - ling, __ Don't Smoke In Bed. __ Good-bye old __ Don't Smoke In Bed. __

DOLPHIN DREAMS

By LEE RITENOUR

DINDI

Music by ANTONIO CARLOS JOBIM
Portuguese Lyrics by ALOYSIO DE OLIVEIRA
English Lyrics by RAY GILBERT

DIPPERMOUTH BLUES

Music by JOSEPH OLIVER

Down Hearted Blues

Words by ALBERTA HUNTER
Music by LOVIE AUSTIN

Additional Choruses (Ad lib.)

Chorus 3: Say, I ain't never loved but three {men/women} in my life.

No, I ain't never loved but three {men/women} in my life,

'Twas my {father, brother/mother, sister} and the {man/woman} who wrecked my life.

Chorus 4: 'Cause {he/she} mistreated me and {he/she} drove me from {his/her} door,

Ye, {he/she} mistreated me and {he/she} drove me from {his/her} door,

But the Good Book says you'll reap just what you sow.

Chorus 5: Oh, it may be a week and it may be a month or two,
Yes, it may be a week and it may be a month or two,
But the day you quit me honey, it's coming home to you.

Chorus 6: Oh, I walked the floor and I wrung my hands and cried,
Yes, I walked the floor and I wrung my hands and cried,
Had the Down Hearted Blues and couldn't be satisfied.

DOWN UNDER

By DIZZY GILLESPIE

DOLPHIN DANCE

By HERBIE HANCOCK

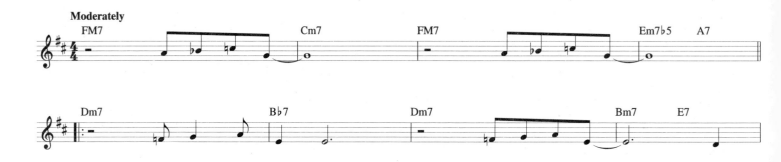

EASY LIVING
Theme from the Paramount Picture EASY LIVING

Words and Music by LEO ROBIN
and RALPH RAINGER

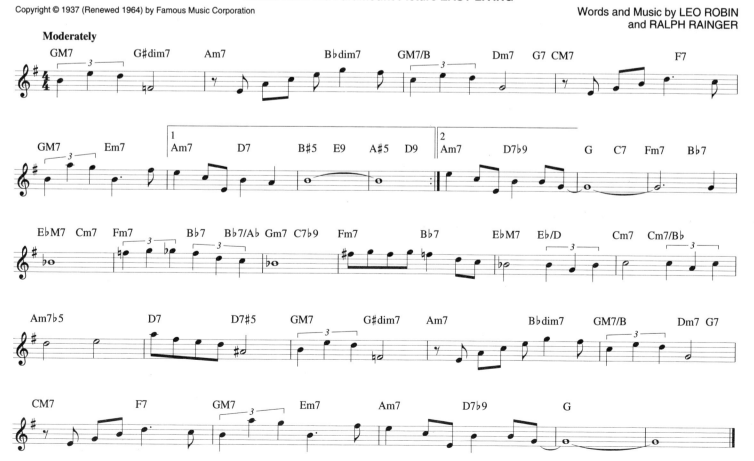

DOWN WITH LOVE
from the Musical Production HOORAY FOR WHAT!

Lyric by E.Y. HARBURG
Music by HAROLD ARLEN

DREAM DANCING

Words and Music by
COLE PORTER

Moderately

When day is gone and night comes on, un-til the dawn what do I do? ___ ___ I clasp your hand and wan-der through slumb-er-land, ___ Dream Danc-ing ___ with you. We dance be-tween a sky se-rene and fields of green, spark-ling with dew. ___ It's joy sub-lime, when-ev-er I spend my time ___ Dream Danc-ing ___ with you. ___ Dream Danc-ing, ___ oh, what a luck-y wind-fall! Touch-ing you, clutch-ing you all ___ the night through. ___ So say you love me dear, and let me make my ca-reer ___ Dream Danc-ing, ___ to par-a-dise pranc-ing, ___ Dream Danc-ing ___ with you. ___ When you. ___

EIGHT

Written by RON CARTER

Moderately fast

EAST ST. LOUIS TOODLE-OO

By DUKE ELLINGTON
and BUB MILEY

DROP ME OFF IN HARLEM

Words by NICK KENNY
Music by DUKE ELLINGTON

EASY DOES IT

Words by SY OLIVER
Music by SY OLIVER and JIMMY YOUNG

EASY RIDER
(I Wonder Where My Easy Rider's Gone)

By SHELTON BROOKS

EASY STREET

By ALAN RANKIN JONES

EL PRINCE

By PAUL DESMOND

With a flowing movement

ELEVEN FOUR

By PAUL DESMOND

EMANCIPATION BLUES

By OLIVER NELSON

EPISTROPHY

By THELONIOUS MONK
and KENNY CLARK

THE END OF INNOCENCE

By BILLY CHILDS

EQUINOX

By JOHN COLTRANE

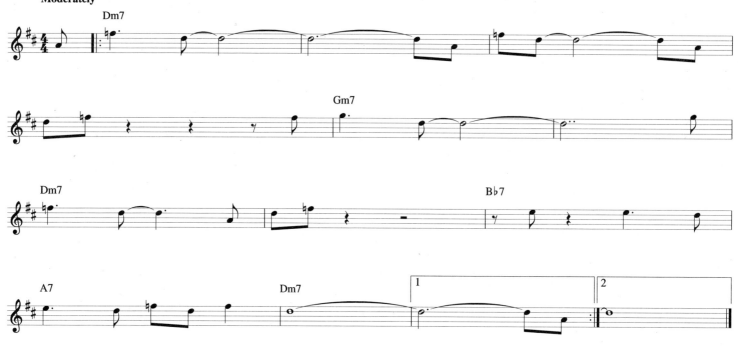

EV'RYTHING I LOVE

Words and Music by
COLE PORTER

ESTATE

Music by BRUNO MARTINO
Lyrics by BRUNO BRIGHETTI

THE FACE I LOVE

Lyric by RAY GILBERT
Music by MARCOS VALLE
Portuguese Lyric by PAULO VALLE and G. PINGARILNO

FALLING GRACE

By STEVE SWALLOW

FALLING IN LOVE

Music by VICTOR FELDMAN

FIRST TRIP

Written by RON CARTER

FILTHY McNASTY

Words and Music by
HORACE SILVER

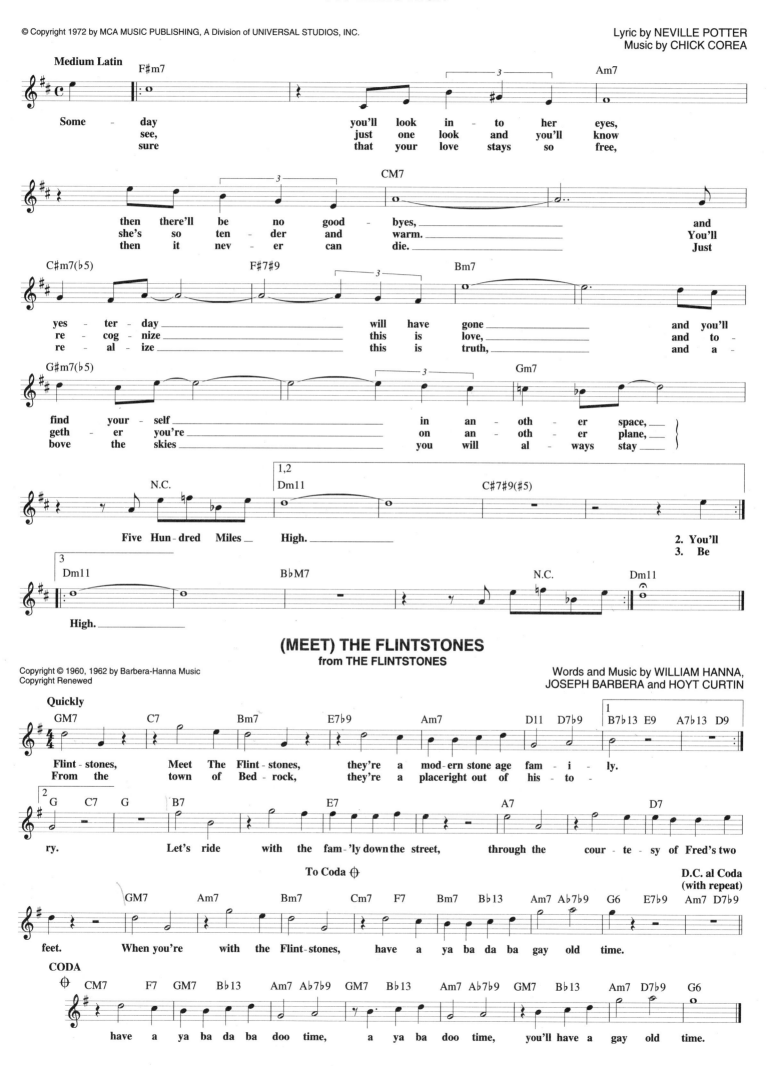

FOUR ON SIX

By JOHN L. "WES" MONTGOMERY

Ten. Sax *8va throughout*

FEELS SO GOOD

By CHUCK MANGIONE

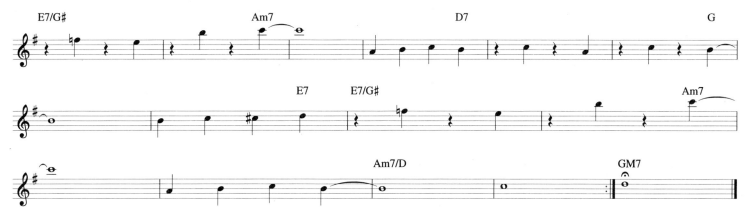

FLANAGAN

By BILLY CHILDS

FLY WITH THE WIND

By McCOY TYNER

THE FOLKS WHO LIVE ON THE HILL
from HIGH, WIDE AND HANDSOME

Lyrics by OSCAR HAMMERSTEIN II
Music by JEROME KERN

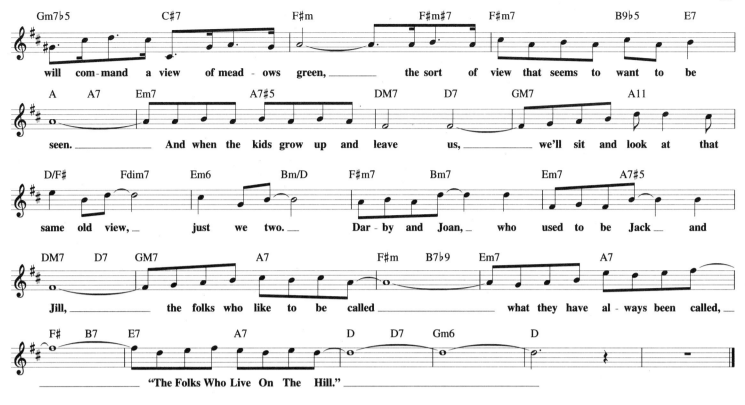

FOR HEAVEN'S SAKE

Words and Music by DON MEYER,
ELISE BRETTON and SHERMAN EDWARDS

FRECKLE FACE

By SAMMY NESTICO

FOREVER IN LOVE

By KENNY G

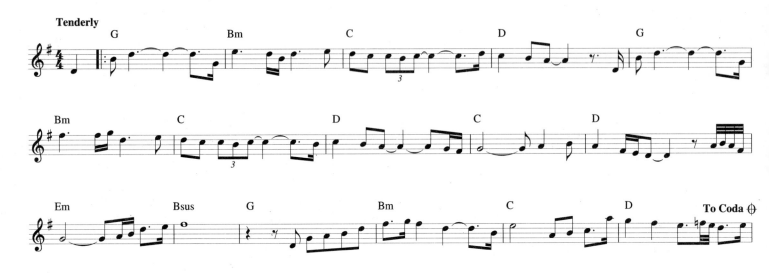

FREEDOM JAZZ DANCE

By EDDIE HARRIS

Medium Funk/Rock

FREETIME

By TOM SCHUMAN
and ELI KONIKOFF

GIANT STEPS

By JOHN COLTRANE

FRENESI

Words and Music by
ALBERTO DOMINGUEZ

FRIENDS

By CHICK COREA

FULL HOUSE

By DAVID SANBORN
and MARCUS MILLER

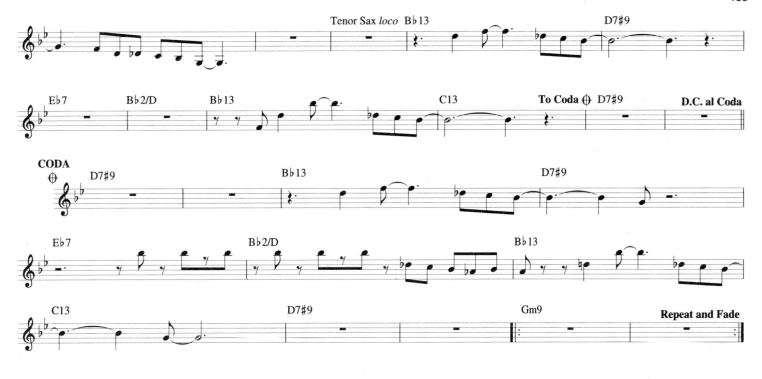

GEORGIA ON MY MIND

Words by STUART GORRELL
Music by HOAGY CARMICHAEL

GETTIN' OVER THE BLUES

Words and Music by PORTIA NELSON
and HAL HACKADY

Moderately slow

There's a song   I don't sing   an-y-more,   there's a
note   that I no   long-er read,   there's a

cock-tail   I won't   drink a-lone.   There's a smile   and a   face____   that I
pho-to   I've turned   to the wall.   There's a   mil-lion and   one____   fool-ish

try   to e-rase,____   and a num-ber   I   try   not to   phone.   Go-in'   my
things   that I've done,____   but they don't seem   to   help   me at   all.   I'm what   you'd

own }   Get-tin'   O-ver   The   Blues._____   There's a
call }

1

Blues._____   I keep liv-ing   it   o-ver   and

2

o-ver   a-gain,   ev-'ry look,   ev-'ry sigh,   ev-'ry kiss.   But the

more   I   re-mem-ber,   the   deep-er the pain.   How could   some-thing   so   won-der-ful

end   like   this?   There are friends   I   don't see   an-y-more,   (Boy)   there are
(Girl)   (There's a

cuff links   I   no   long-er wear.   There's a   lit-tle ca-fe____   I go
flow-er)

out   of my   way____   to a-void   on the chance   she'll   be   there.   But what-

ev-er   I   do,   it's   in-creas-ing-ly   true   that a   torch   is   a one   way   af-

GODCHILD

Composed by
GEORGE WALLINGTON

GIRL TALK
from the Paramount Picture HARLOW

Words by BOBBY TROUP
Music by NEAL HEFTI

GLAD TO BE UNHAPPY
from ON YOUR TOES

Words by LORENZ HART
Music by RICHARD RODGERS

GOOD-BYE

Words and Music by
GORDON JENKINS

GOING HOME

By KENNY G
and WALTER AFANASIEFF

GOOD MORNING HEARTACHE

Words and Music by DAN FISHER,
IRENE HIGGINBOTHAM and ERVIN DRAKE

GRAVY WALTZ

Lyrics by STEVE ALLEN
Music by RAY BROWN

GREENS

By BENNY GREEN

GREEN EYES
(Aquellos Ojos Verdes)

Words and Music by ADOLFO UTRERA
and NILO MENDEZ

Moderately

Your Green Eyes with their soft lights, _____ Your eyes that prom-ise sweet nights _____
A - que - llos o - jos ver - des _____ de mi - ra - da se - re - na _____

___ Bring to my soul a long - ing _____ a thirst for love di - vine. _____
___ De - ja - ron en mi al - ma eter - na sed de a - mar _____

___ In dreams I seem to hold you _____ To find you and en - fold you _____
___ An - he - los de ca - ri - cias _____ de be - sos y ter - nu - ras _____

___ Our lips meet, and our hearts too, _____ with a thrill so sub - lime. _____
de to - das las dul - zu - ras _____ que sa - bi - an brin - dar _____

___ Those cool and lim - pid Green Eyes _____ A pool where - in my love lies _____
___ A - que - llos o - jos ver - des _____ se - re - nos co - mo un la - go _____

___ so deep, that in my search - ing _____ For hap - pi - ness, I fear _____
___ en cu - yas quie - tas a - guas _____ un di - a me mi - ré _____

___ That they will ev - er haunt me _____ All through my life they'll taunt me ___
___ No sa - ben las tris - te - zas _____ que en mi al - ma han de - ja - do

But will they ev - er want me _____ Green Eyes make my dreams come
A - que - llos o - jos ver - des _____ que yo nun - ca be - sa -

1

true.
ré.

Your Green Eyes with their true. _____
A - que - llos o - jos ré. _____

2

GUESS I'LL HANG MY TEARS OUT TO DRY
from GLAD TO SEE YOU

Words by SAMMY CAHN
Music by JULE STYNE

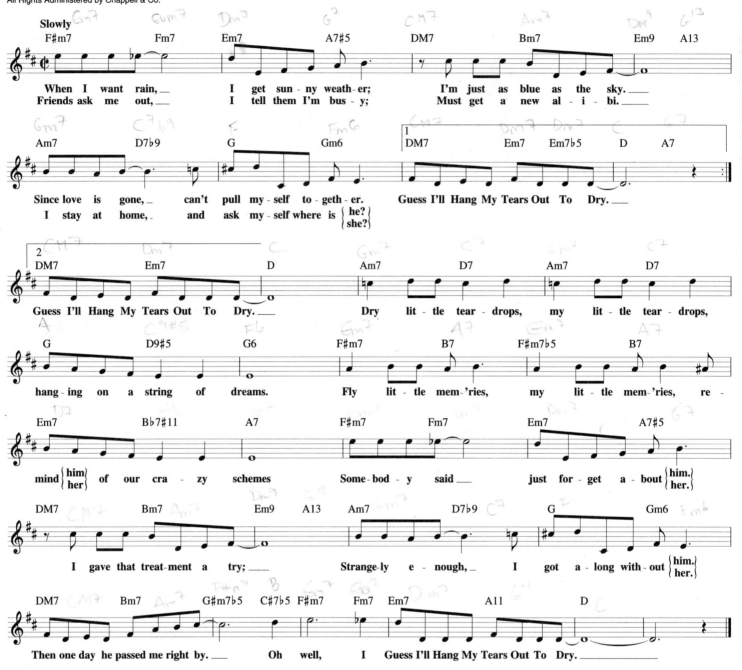

When I want rain, ___ I get sun-ny weath-er; I'm just as blue as the sky. ___
Friends ask me out, ___ I tell them I'm bus-y; Must get a new al-i-bi. ___

Since love is gone, ___ can't pull my-self to-geth-er. Guess I'll Hang My Tears Out To Dry. ___
I stay at home, ___ and ask my-self where is { he? / she? }

Guess I'll Hang My Tears Out To Dry. ___ Dry lit-tle tear-drops, my lit-tle tear-drops,

hang-ing on a string of dreams. Fly lit-tle mem-'ries, my lit-tle mem-'ries, re-

mind { him / her } of our cra-zy schemes Some-bod-y said ___ just for-get a-bout { him. / her. }

I gave that treat-ment a try; ___ Strange-ly e-nough, ___ I got a-long with-out { him. / her. }

Then one day he passed me right by. ___ Oh well, I Guess I'll Hang My Tears Out To Dry. ___

GROWING

By JOHN PATITUCCI

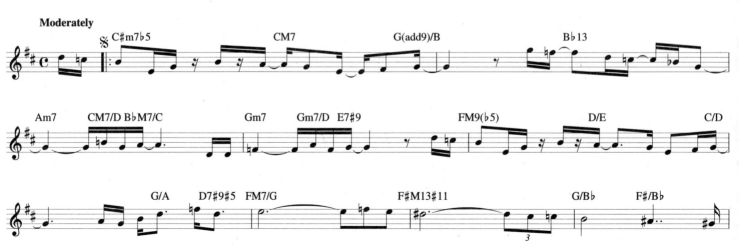

HAPPY WITH THE BLUES

Lyric by PEGGY LEE
Music by HAROLD ARLEN

THE HAWK TALKS

By LOUIS BELLSON

HAPPY HUNTING HORN
from PAL JOEY

Words by LORENZ HART
Music by RICHARD RODGERS

Dan - ger's eas - y to en - dure when you're out to catch a beaut; __ Lie in am - bush but be sure, when you see the whites of their eyes, don't shoot! Play the horn from night to morn, just play, no __ mat - ter what time. __ Play "There'll __ be a hot time" hap - py lit - tle hunt (Bang! Bang!) - ing horn! horn! _____

HELEN'S SONG

By GEORGE CABLES

HEEBIE JEEBIES

By BOYD ATKINS

HERE'S TO MY LADY

Lyric by JOHNNY MERCER
Music by RUBE BLOOM

Hideaway

By DAVID SANBORN

HERE'S TO YOUR ILLUSIONS

Words and Music by SAMMY FAIN
and E.Y. HARBURG

HONEST I DO

By JIMMY REED
and EWART G. ABNER, JR.

stop driv-ing me mad.. You're the sweet-est __ lit-tle wom-an that I ev — er

had. Please tell me you love __ me, __ stop driv-ing me mad. __

When I woke __ up this morn-ing nev-er felt _____ so bad.

HOW ABOUT ME?

Words and Music by
IRVING BERLIN

Slowly

It's o-ver, all o-ver, and soon some-bod-y else __ will

make a fuss __ a-bout you, but How __ A-bout Me? _____

It's o-ver, all o-ver, and soon some-bod-y else __ will

tell his friends __ a-bout you, but How __ A-bout Me? _____ You'll find some —

bod-y new, __ but what am I to do? __ I'll still re —

mem-ber you __ when you __ have for-got — ten.

And may-be a ba-by will climb up-on your knee __ and

put it's arms __ a-bout you, but How __ A-bout Me? __

HOT TODDY

Words and Music by HERB HENDLER
and RALPH FLANAGAN

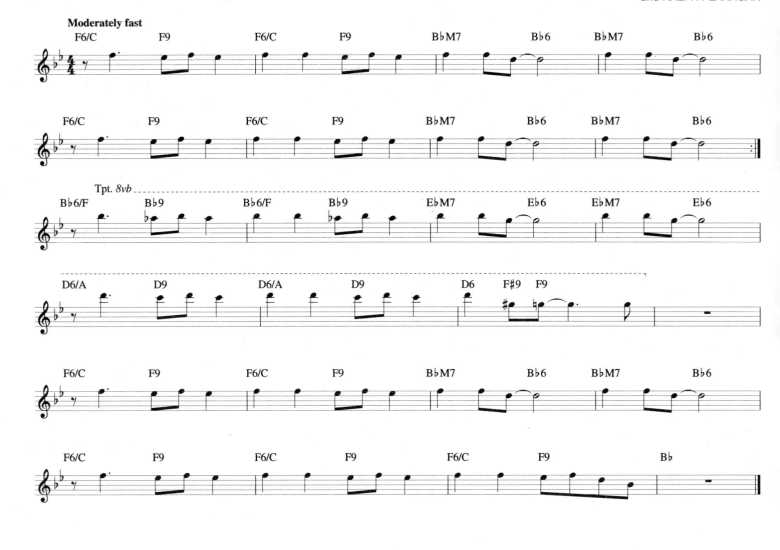

HOW ARE THINGS IN GLOCCA MORRA
from FINIAN'S RAINBOW

Words by E.Y. HARBURG
Music by BURTON LANE

HOW DEEP IS THE OCEAN
(How High Is the Sky)

Words and Music by
IRVING BERLIN

Slowly

HOW MY HEART SINGS

Lyrics by ANNE ZINDARS
Music by EARL ZINDARS

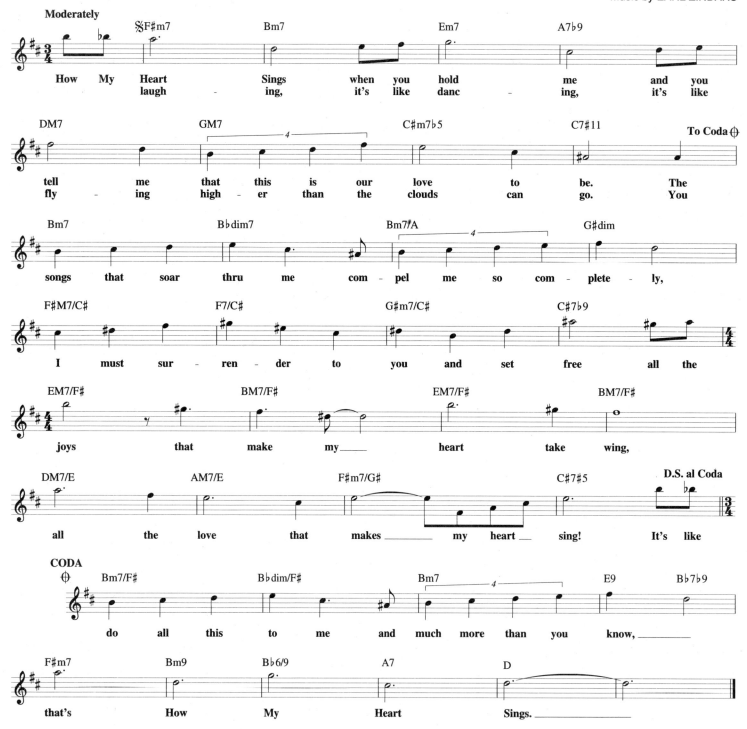

THE HUCKLEBUCK

Lyrics by ROY ALFRED
Music by ANDY GIBSON

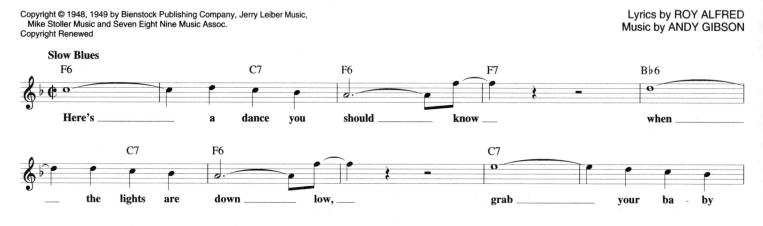

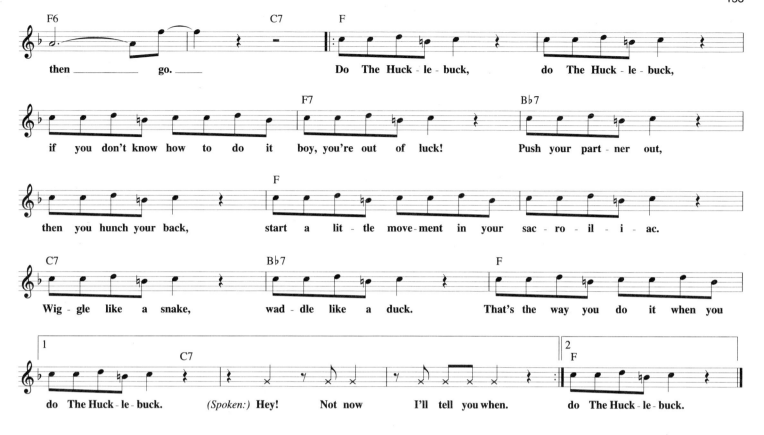

A HUNDRED YEARS FROM TODAY
from LEW LESLIE'S BLACKBIRDS OF 1934

Lyric by JOE YOUNG and NED WASHINGTON
Music by VICTOR YOUNG

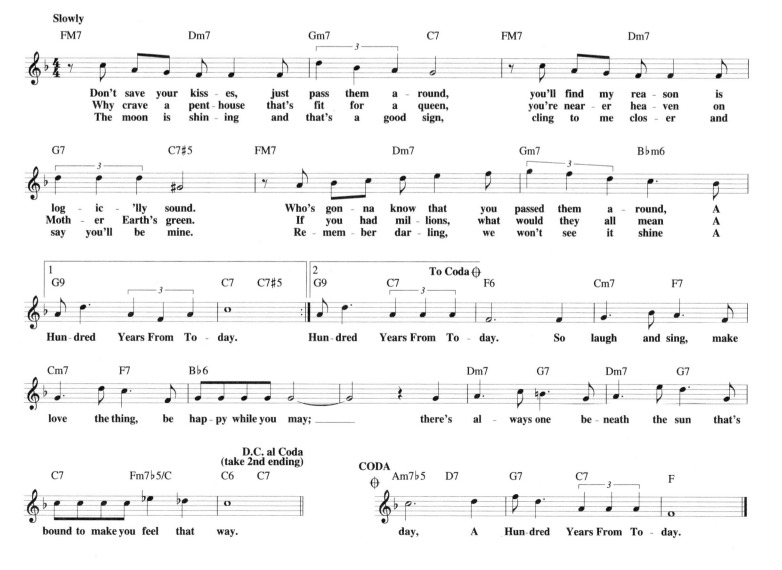

HYPNOSIS

Written by JOE LOVANO

I AIN'T GOT NOTHIN' BUT THE BLUES

Words by DON GEORGE
Music by DUKE ELLINGTON

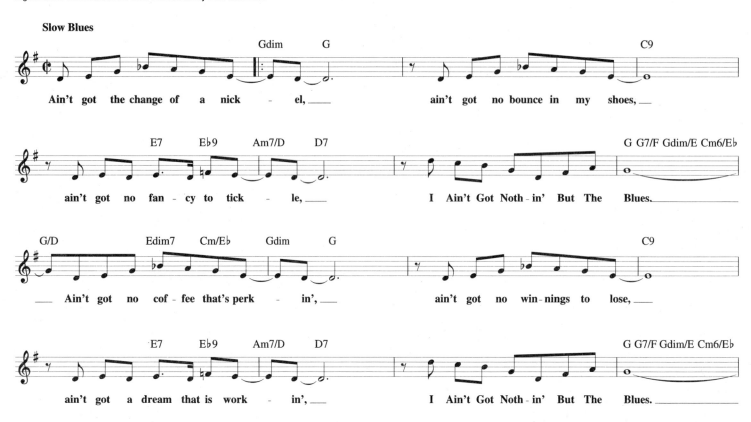

I CAN'T BELIEVE THAT YOU'RE IN LOVE WITH ME

Words and Music by JIMMY McHUGH
and CLARENCE GASKILL

I AM IN LOVE
from CAN-CAN

Words and Music by
COLE PORTER

I GOT IT BAD AND THAT AIN'T GOOD

Words by PAUL FRANCIS WEBSTER
Music by DUKE ELLINGTON

I HEAR MUSIC
from the Paramount Picture DANCING ON A DIME

Words by FRANK LOESSER
Music by BURTON LANE

I DIDN'T KNOW ABOUT YOU

Words by BOB RUSSELL
Music by DUKE ELLINGTON

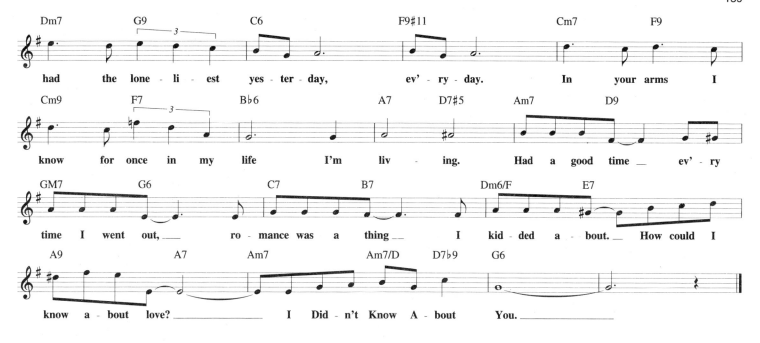

I GET ALONG WITHOUT YOU VERY WELL
(Except Sometimes)

Words and Music by HOAGY CARMICHAEL
Inspired by a poem written by J.B. THOMPSON

I LET A SONG GO OUT OF MY HEART

Words and Music by DUKE ELLINGTON, HENRY NEMO,
JOHN REDMOND and IRVING MILLS

Moderately

I Let a Song_ Go Out Of My Heart, It was the sweet-est mel-o-dy,_ I know I ___ lost heav-
Since you and I ___ have drift-ed a-part life does-n't mean a thing to me,_ Please come back_ sweet mu-

-en ___ 'Cause you were the song. know I was wrong. ___ Am I too
-sic. ___ I

late _____ to make a-mends. _____ You know that we were meant to be more than just

friends, just friends._ I Let A Song_ Go Out Of My Heart, Be-lieve me, dar-ling,

when I say _ I won't know_ sweet mu - sic un-til you re-turn some day. day.

I GOT YOU
(I Feel Good)

Words and Music by
JAMES BROWN

Moderately
Tpt. 8vb throughout

Woh! I feel good. _ I knew that I would_ now. I feel ___
___ Ah, sug-ar and spice ___ I feel ___

___ good. I knew that I would_ now. So good, so good,
___ nice. Ah, sug-ar and spice. So nice, so nice,

To Coda

I Got _ You. Whoa! I feel nice.
I Got _ You.

When I hold you _ in my arms I

know that I can do no wrong. _ And when I hold you in ___ my arms my

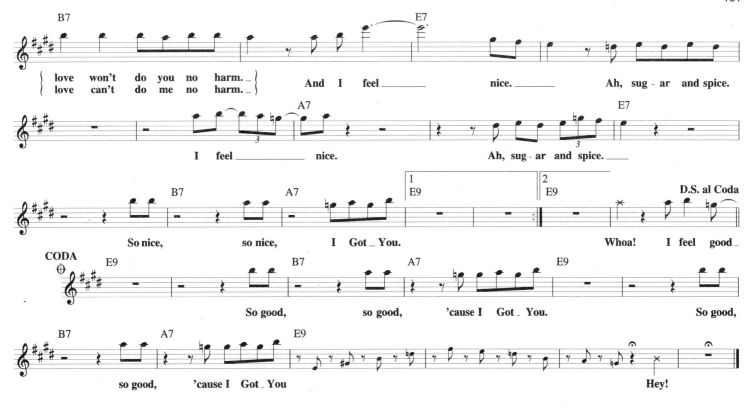

I GOTTA RIGHT TO SING THE BLUES

Words by TED KOEHLER
Music by HAROLD ARLEN

I KEEP GOING BACK TO JOE'S

Words and Music by MARVIN FISHER
and JACK SEGAL

I LEFT THIS SPACE FOR YOU

Written by ARTURO SANDOVAL

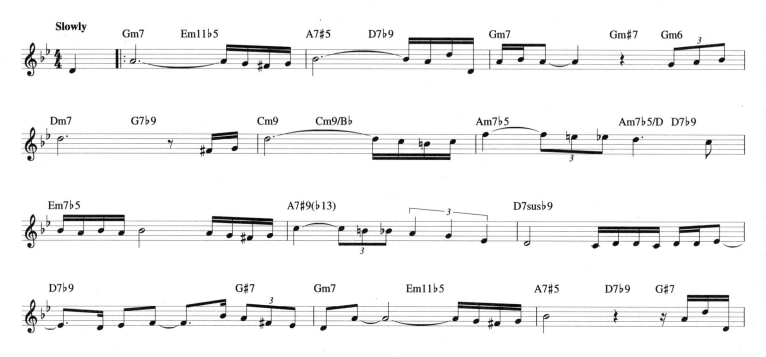

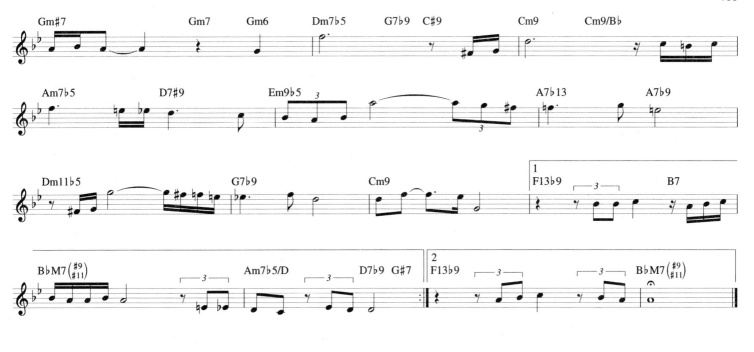

I MEAN YOU

By THELONIOUS MONK
and COLEMAN HAWKINS

I REMEMBER BIRD

By LEONARD FEATHER

I REMEMBER YOU
from the Paramount Picture THE FLEET'S IN

Words by JOHNNY MERCER
Music by VICTOR SCHERTZINGER

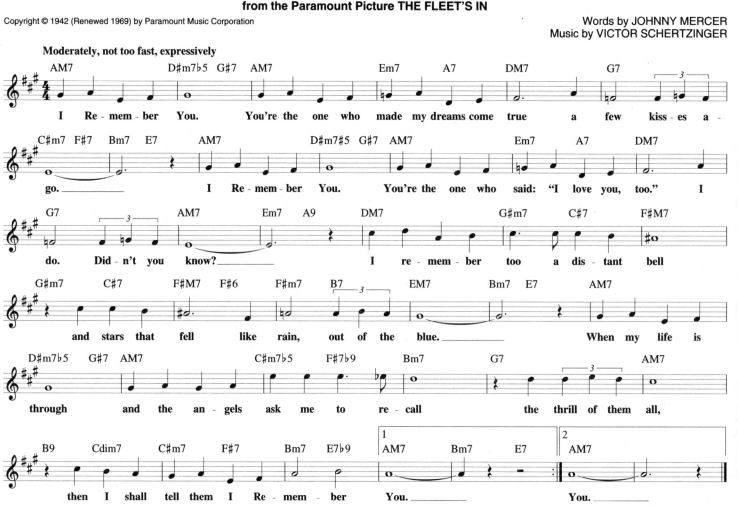

I THOUGHT ABOUT YOU

Words by JOHNNY MERCER
Music by JIMMY VAN HEUSEN

IF I SHOULD LOSE YOU
from the Paramount Picture ROSE OF THE RANCHO

Words and Music by LEO ROBIN
and RALPH RAINGER

I TOLD YA I LOVE YA NOW GET OUT

By JOHN FRIGO, LOU CARTER
and HERB ELLIS

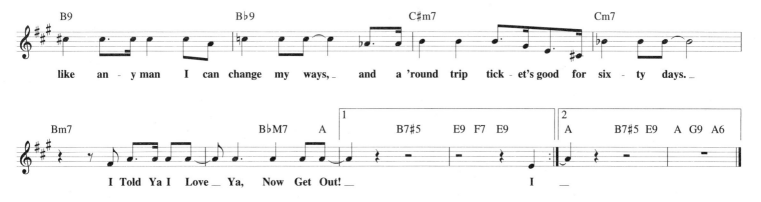

like an-y man I can change my ways, and a 'round trip tick-et's good for six-ty days.

I Told Ya I Love Ya, Now Get Out! I

I WATCHED HER WALK AWAY

By RUSS FREEMAN

Moderate Jazz Rock

I WISH I WERE IN LOVE AGAIN
from BABES IN ARMS

Words by LORENZ HART
Music by RICHARD RODGERS

I WISHED ON THE MOON

Words and Music by DOROTHY PARKER
and RALPH RAINGER

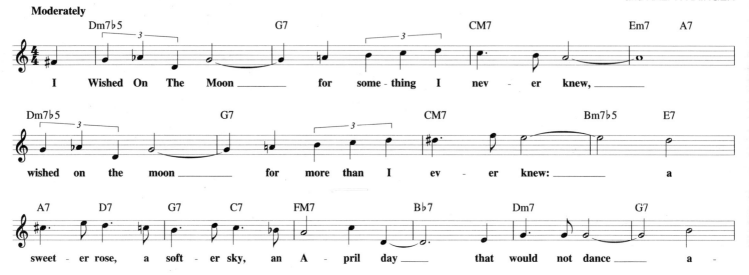

way. _____ I begged of a star _____ to throw me a beam or two, _____ wished on a star _____ and asked for a dream or two. _____ I looked for ev - 'ry love - li - ness, it all came true; ___ I Wished On The Moon _____ for you. _____

IF YOU GO

French Lyrics and Music by MICHEL EMER
English Lyrics by GEOFFREY PARSONS

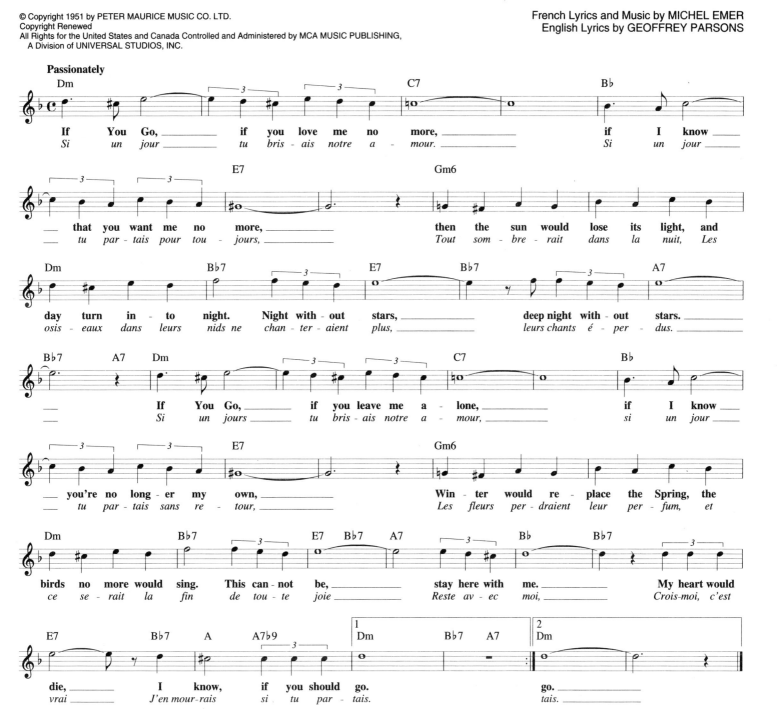

If You Go, _____ if you love me no more, _____ if I know _____
Si un jour _____ tu bris - ais notre a - mour. _____ Si un jour _____

___ that you want me no more, _____ then the sun would lose its light, and
___ tu par - tais pour tou - jours, _____ Tout som - bre - rait dans la nuit, Les

day turn in - to night. Night with - out stars, _____ deep night with - out stars.
osis - eaux dans leurs nids ne chan - ter - aient plus, _____ leurs chants é - per - dus.

___ If You Go, _____ if you leave me a - lone, _____ if I know _____
___ Si un jours _____ tu bris - ais notre a - mour, _____ si un jour _____

___ you're no long - er my own, _____ Win - ter would re - place the Spring, the
___ tu par - tais sans re - tour, _____ Les fleurs per - draient leur per - fum, et

birds no more would sing. This can - not be, _____ stay here with me. _____ My heart would
ce se - rait la fin de tou - te joie Reste av - ec moi, Crois-moi, c'est

die, _____ I know, if you should go. go. _____
vrai J'en mour - rais si tu par - tais. tais.

IF WE MEET AGAIN, PART ONE

By AL DI MEOLA

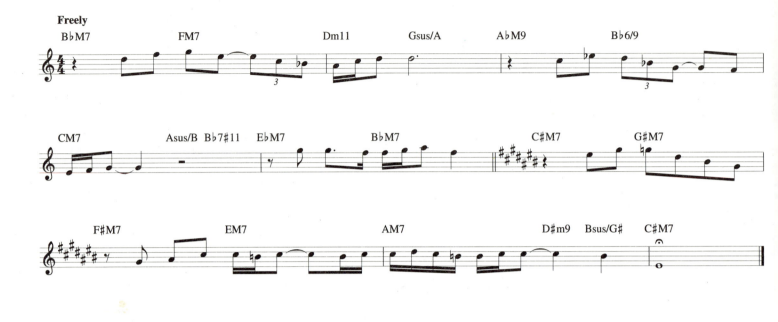

IF YOU NEVER COME TO ME
(Inutil paisagem)

Music by ANTONIO CARLOS JOBIM
Portuguese Lyrics by ALOYSIO DE OLIVEIRA
English Lyrics by RAY GILBERT

I'LL BUILD A STAIRWAY TO PARADISE

Words by B.G. DeSYLVA and IRA GERSHWIN
Music by GEORGE GERSHWIN

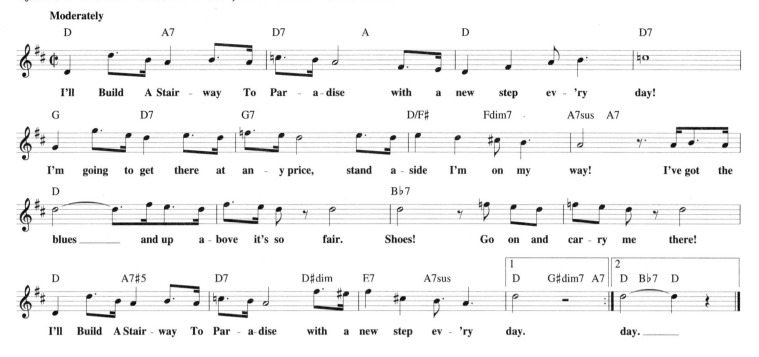

I'M A FOOL TO WANT YOU

Words and Music by JACK WOLF,
JOEL HERRON and FRANK SINATRA

I'LL CLOSE MY EYES

By BUDDY KAYE
and BILLY REID

I'M ALL SMILES
from THE YEARLING

Lyric by HERBERT MARTIN
Music by MICHAEL LEONARD

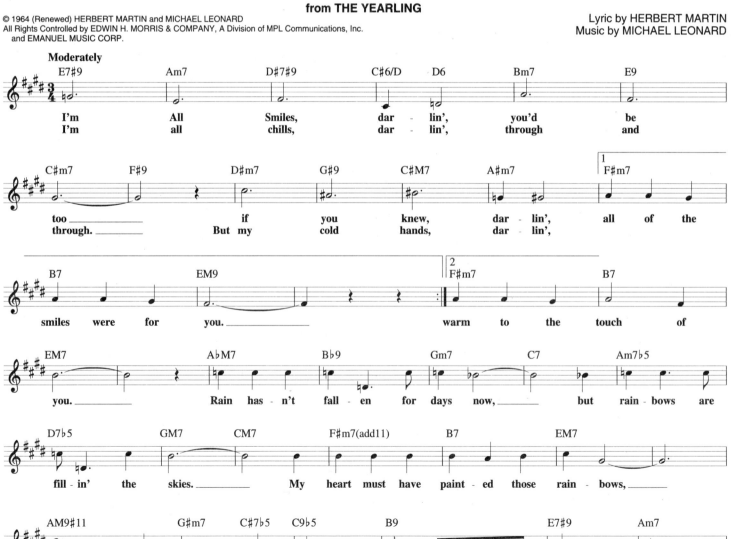

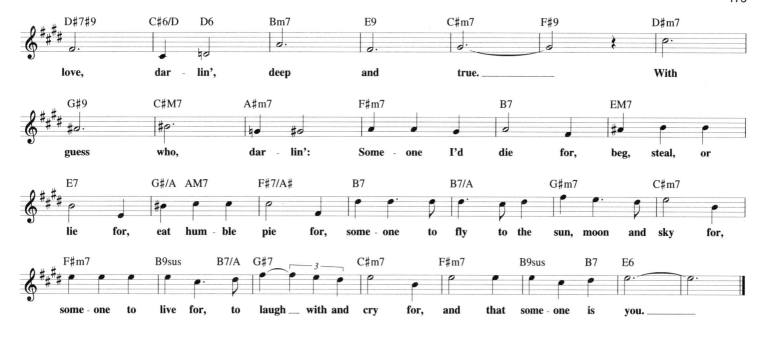

I'M JUST A LUCKY SO AND SO

Words by MACK DAVID
Music by DUKE ELLINGTON

I'M A DREAMER AREN'T WE ALL

Words and Music by B.G. DeSYLVA,
LEW BROWN and RAY HENDERSON

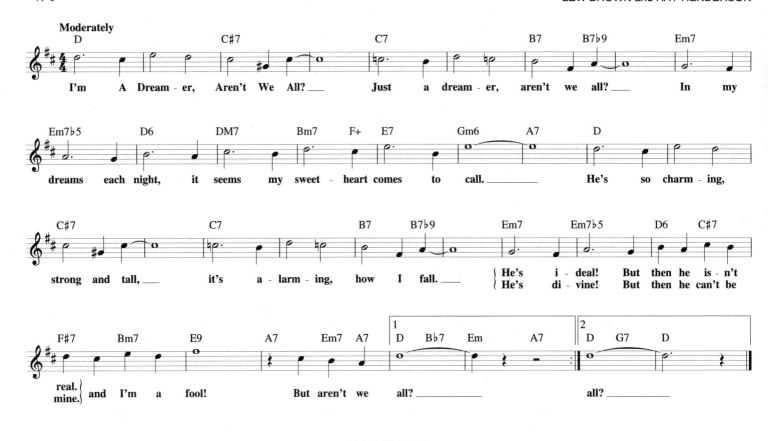

I'M YOURS
from the Paramount Picture Short LEAVE IT TO LESTER

Words by E.Y. HARBURG
Music by JOHNNY GREEN

I'M GONNA GO FISHIN'

Words and Music by DUKE ELLINGTON
and PEGGY LEE

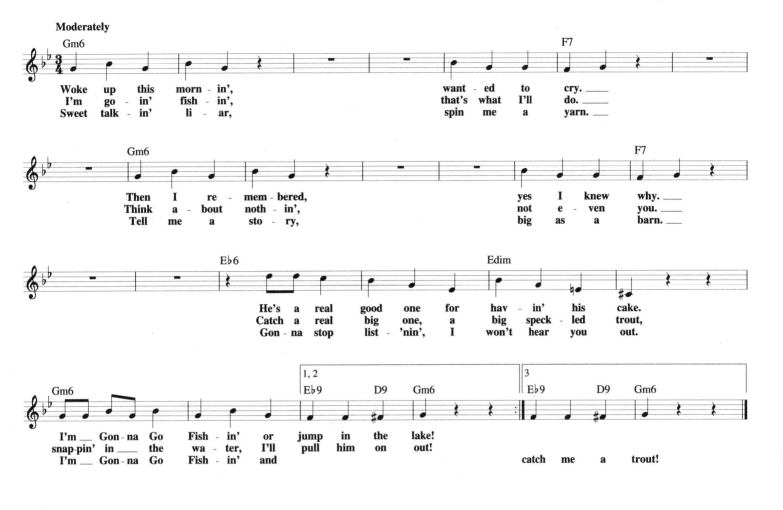

Moderately

Woke up this morn - in', want - ed to cry.
I'm go - in' fish - in', that's what I'll do.
Sweet talk - in' li - ar, spin me a yarn.

Then I re - mem - bered, yes I knew why.
Think a - bout noth - in', not e - ven you.
Tell me a sto - ry, big as a barn.

He's a real good one for hav - in' his cake.
Catch a real big one, a big speck - led trout,
Gon - na stop list - 'nin', I won't hear you out.

I'm __ Gon - na Go Fish - in' or jump in the lake!
snap - pin' in __ the wa - ter, I'll pull him on out!
I'm __ Gon - na Go Fish - in' and catch me a trout!

IMPRESSIONS

By JOHN COLTRANE

Fast Swing

To Coda ⊕   D.C. al Coda

CODA

IN A SENTIMENTAL MOOD

Words and Music by DUKE ELLINGTON,
IRVING MILLS and MANNY KURTZ

IN LOVE IN VAIN

Words by LEO ROBIN
Music by JEROME KERN

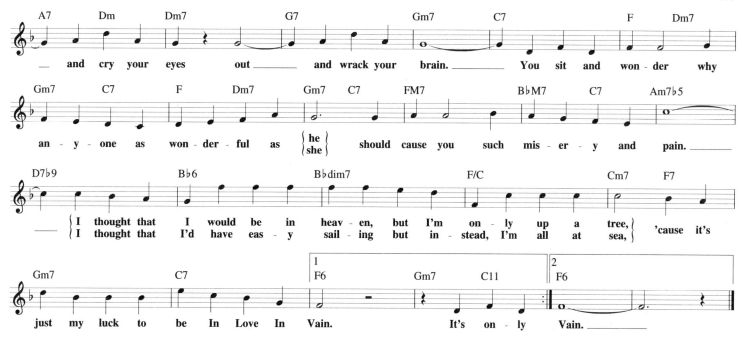

IN THE COOL, COOL, COOL OF THE EVENING
from the Paramount Picture HERE COMES THE GROOM

Words by JOHNNY MERCER
Music by HOAGY CARMICHAEL

IN THE LAND OF EPHESUS

Written by JOE LOVANO

IN THE WEE SMALL HOURS OF THE MORNING

Words by BOB HILLIARD
Music by DAVID MANN

IN WALKED BUD

By THELONIOUS MONK

INSIDE

Written by KEVIN EUBANKS

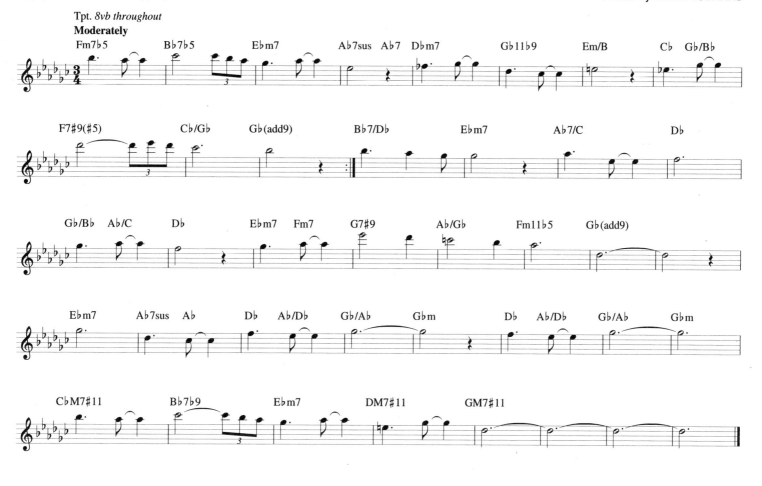

THE INTREPID FOX

By FREDDIE HUBBARD

INSIDE OUT

By RANDY BRECKER

INVITATION

Words by PAUL FRANCIS WEBSTER
Music by BRONISLAU KAPER

ISREAL

© 1954 (Renewed 1982) BEECHWOOD MUSIC CORP.

By JOHN CARISI

IT DON'T MEAN A THING
(If It Ain't Got That Swing)
from SOPHISTICATED LADIES

Copyright © 1932 (Renewed 1959) and Assigned to Famous Music Corporation and EMI Mills Music Inc. in the U.S.A.
Rights for the world outside the U.S.A. Controlled by EMI Mills Music Inc. and Warner Bros. Publications Inc.

Words and Music by DUKE ELLINGTON
and IRVING MILLS

IS IT YOU?

By LEE RITENOUR,
ERIC TAGG and BILL CHAMPLIN

'cause it's way too late to run a way. ___ Don't run
a way from love, _____ my ___ love. Is It You?

CODA

Is It You _____

knock - in' on _____ my door? _____ Is it my i -

mag - i - na - tion? _____ Is It You I can't ___

___ get off _____ my mind? _____ Is ___ It

You, _____ you, _____ you? _____

ISN'T IT ROMANTIC?
from the Paramount Picture LOVE ME TONIGHT

Copyright © 1932 (Renewed 1959) by Famous Music Corporation

Words by LORENZ HART
Music by RICHARD RODGERS

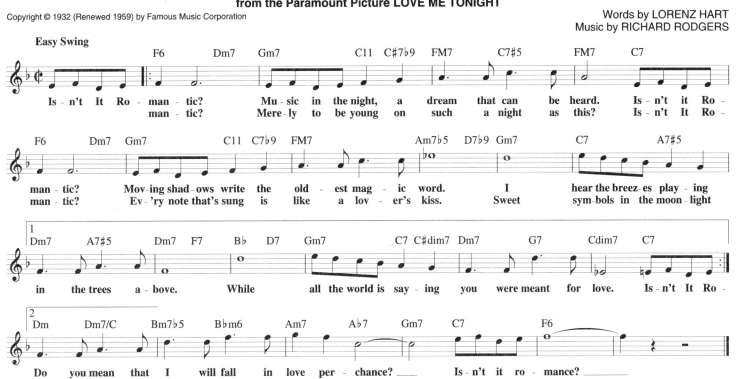

Is - n't It Ro - man - tic? Mu - sic in the night, a dream that can be heard. Is - n't it Ro -
man - tic? Mere - ly to be young on such a night as this? Is - n't It Ro -

man - tic? Mov - ing shad - ows write the old - est mag - ic word. I hear the breez - es play - ing
man - tic? Ev - 'ry note that's sung is like a lov - er's kiss. Sweet sym - bols in the moon - light

in the trees a - bove. While all the world is say - ing you were meant for love. Is - n't It Ro -

Do you mean that I will fall in love per - chance? ___ Is - n't it ro - mance?

IT COULD HAPPEN TO YOU
from the Paramount Picture AND THE ANGELS SING

Words by JOHNNY BURKE
Music by JAMES VAN HEUSEN

IT'S A LOVELY DAY TODAY
from the Stage Production CALL ME MADAM

Words and Music by
IRVING BERLIN

IT ONLY HAPPENS WHEN I DANCE WITH YOU
from the Motion Picture Irving Berlin's EASTER PARADE

Words and Music by
IRVING BERLIN

IT'S EASY TO REMEMBER
from the Paramount Picture MISSISSIPPI

Words by LORENZ HART
Music by RICHARD RODGERS

IT'S YOU

Written by DAVID SANBORN

IT'S YOU OR NO ONE
from ROMANCE ON THE HIGH SEAS

Words by SAMMY CAHN
Music by JULE STYNE

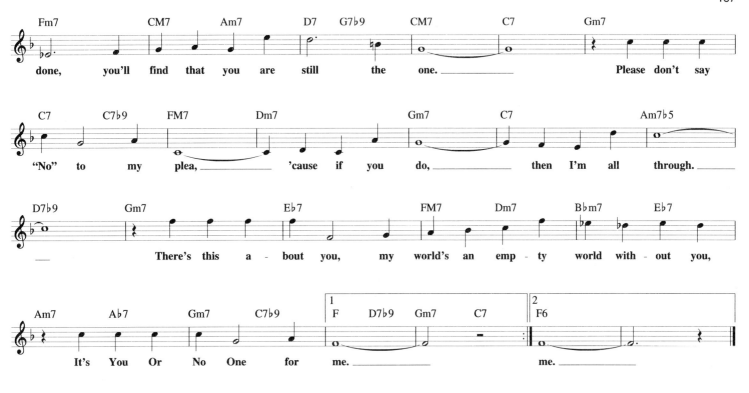

I'VE FOUND A NEW BABY
(I Found A New Baby)

Words and Music by JACK PALMER
and SPENCER WILLIAMS

JAZZMANIA

By BILLY CHILDS

I'VE GOT MY LOVE TO KEEP ME WARM
from the 20th Century Fox Motion Picture ON THE AVENUE

Words and Music by
IRVING BERLIN

Bright jump tempo

The snow is snow-ing, the wind is blow-ing, but I can weath-er the storm.
can't re-mem-ber a worse De-cem-ber; just watch those i-ci-cles form.

What do I care how much it may storm? I've Got My Love To Keep Me Warm.
What do I care if i-ci-cles form?

I

Off with my o-ver-coat, off with my glove.

I need no o-ver-coat, I'm burn-ing with love. My heart's on fire, the

flame grows high-er. So I will weath-er the storm. What do I care how

much it may storm? I've Got My Love To Keep Me Warm.

I'VE GOT THE WORLD ON A STRING

Lyric by TED KOEHLER
Music by HAROLD ARLEN

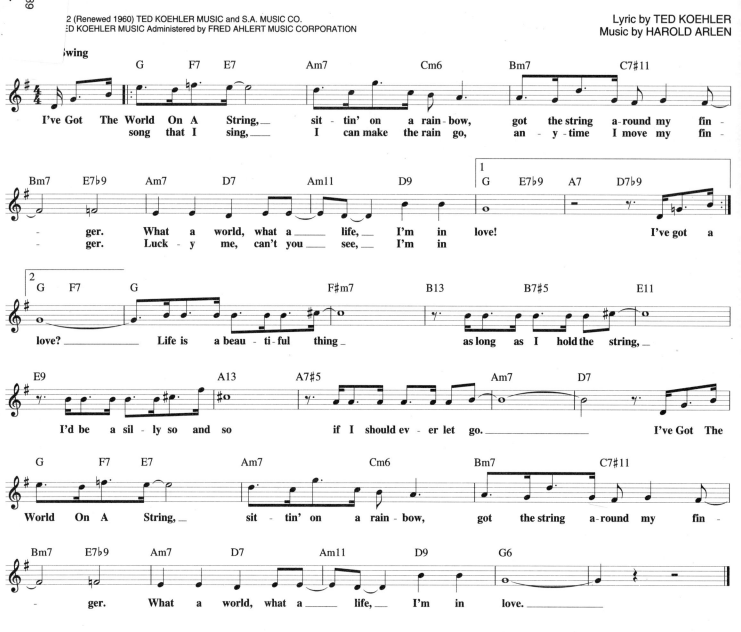

JOSIE AND ROSIE

Written by JOE LOVANO

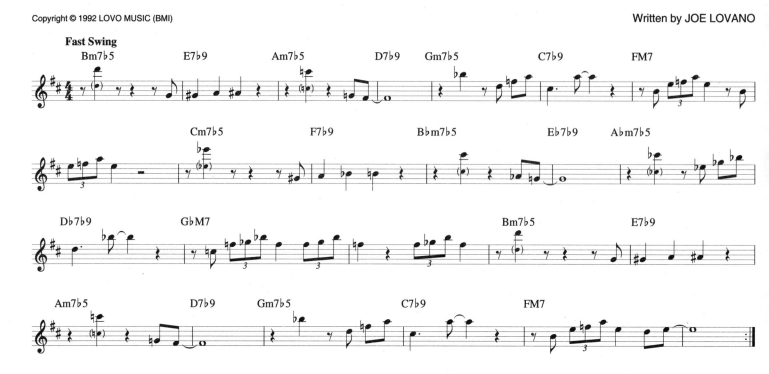

JITTERBUG WALTZ

Music by THOMAS "FATS" WALLER

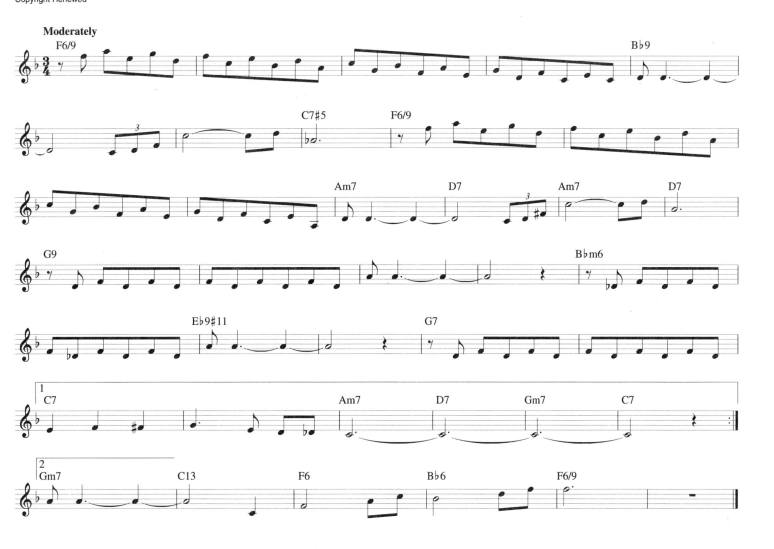

JUST A GIGOLO

Original German Text by JULIUS BRAMMER
English Words by IRVING CAESAR
Music by LEONELLO CASUCCI

JULY

By AL DI MEOLA

Moderately fast

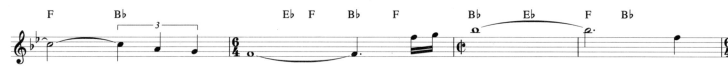

193

JUNE BUG

Music by THOMAS TURRENTINE

JUST ONE MORE CHANCE

Words by SAM COSLOW
Music by ARTHUR JOHNSTON

JUNE IN JANUARY
from the Paramount Picture HERE IS MY HEART

Words and Music by LEO ROBIN
and RALPH RAINGER

It's June In Jan-u-ar-y be-cause I'm in love; it al-ways is spring in my heart, with you in my arms. The snow is just white blos-soms that fall from a-bove, and here is the rea-son my dear, your mag-i-cal charms. The night is cold the trees are bare but I can feel the scent of ros-es in the air. It's June In Jan-u-ar-y be-cause I'm in love, but on-ly be-cause I'm in love with you.

JUST THE WAY WE PLANNED IT

By ERNIE WATTS
and BOB LEATHERBARROW

KEEPIN' OUT OF MISCHIEF NOW

Lyric by ANDY RAZAF
Music by THOMAS "FATS" WALLER

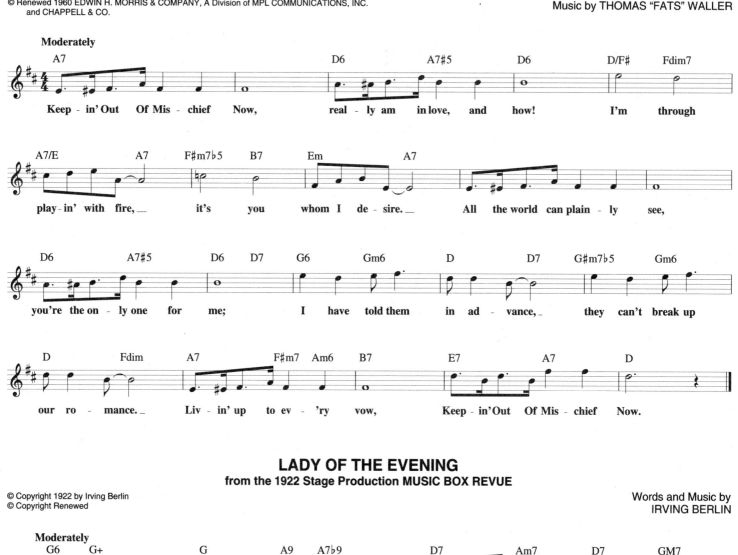

LADY OF THE EVENING
from the 1922 Stage Production MUSIC BOX REVUE

Words and Music by
IRVING BERLIN

KOGUN

By TOSHIKO AKIYOSHI

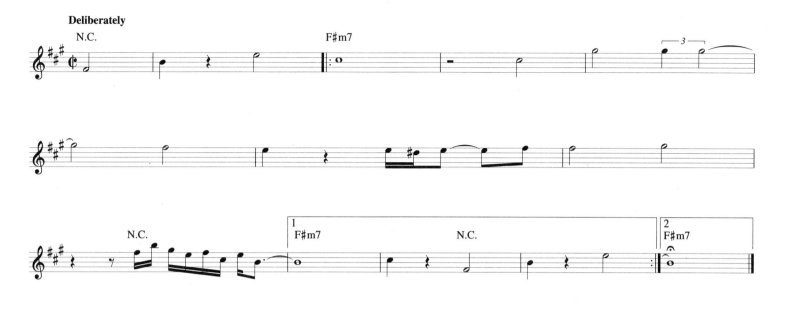

LADY SINGS THE BLUES

Words and Music by HERBERT NICHOLS
and BILLIE HOLIDAY

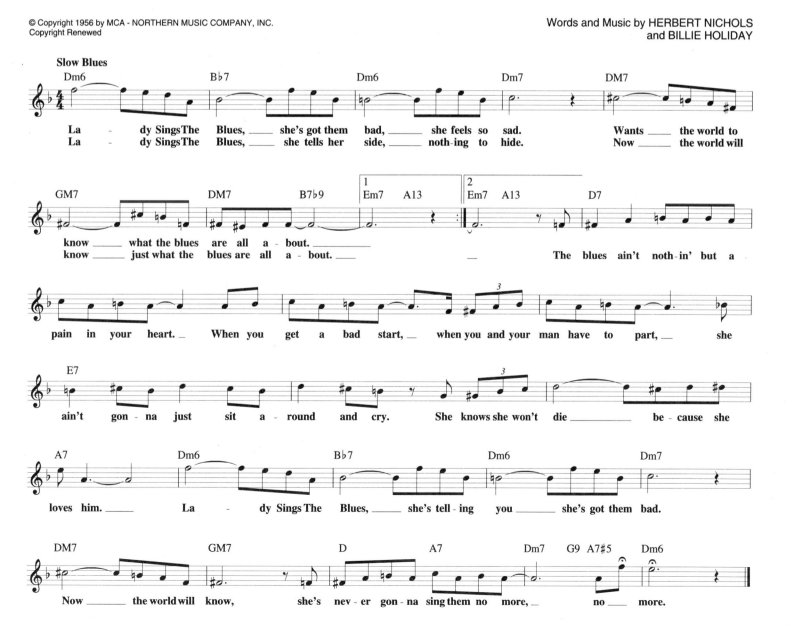

THE LADY'S IN LOVE WITH YOU
from the Paramount Picture SOME LIKE IT HOT

Words by FRANK LOESSER
Music by BURTON LANE

If there's a gleam in her eye ___ each time she straight-ens your tie, ___ you'll know The La-dy's In Love ___ With You. If she can dress for a date ___ with-out that wait-ing you hate ___ it means The La-dy's In Love ___ With You. And when your friends ask you o-ver to join their ta- ble ___ but she picks that far-a-way booth for two, well, sir, here's just how it stands, you've got ro-mance on your hands ___ be-cause The La-dy's In Love ___ With You. If there's a You. ___

LAZY

Words and Music by
IRVING BERLIN

La-zy. ___ I want ___ to be La-zy. ___ I long ___ to be out in the sun ___ with no work to be done, ___ un-der that awn-ing ___ they call the sky, ___ stretch-ing and yawn-ing ___ and let the world ___ go drift-ing by. ___ I wan-na peep through the deep ___ tan-gled wild ___ wood, ___ count-ing sheep ___ 'til I sleep ___ like a child ___ would, ___ with a great big va-lise full of books to read ___ where it's peace-ful, while I'm kill-ing time ___ be-ing La- zy. zy.

LAST NIGHT WHEN WE WERE YOUNG

Lyric by E.Y. HARBURG
Music by HAROLD ARLEN

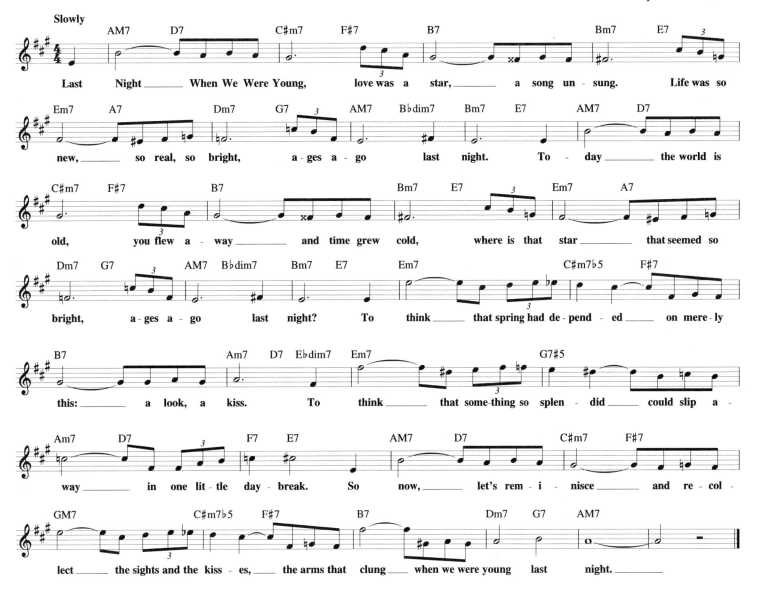

LET'S GET LOST

from the Paramount Picture HAPPY GO LUCKY

Words by FRANK LOESSER
Music by JIMMY McHUGH

LIVELY UP YOURSELF

Words and Music by
BOB MARLEY

LET'S FACE THE MUSIC AND DANCE
from the Motion Picture FOLLOW THE FLEET

Words and Music by
IRVING BERLIN

LINES AND SPACES

Written by JOE LOVANO

LITTLE WHITE LIES

Words and Music by
WALTER DONALDSON

LOVE IS JUST AROUND THE CORNER
from the Paramount Picture HERE IS MY HEART

Words and Music by LEO ROBIN
and LEWIS E. GENSLER

LOOK TO THE SKY

Copyright © 1967, 1968 by Antonio Carlos Jobim
Copyright Renewed

By ANTONIO CARLOS JOBIM

LOVE LETTERS
Theme from the Paramount Picture LOVE LETTERS

Copyright © 1945 (Renewed 1972) by Famous Music Corporation

Words by EDWARD HEYMAN
Music by VICTOR YOUNG

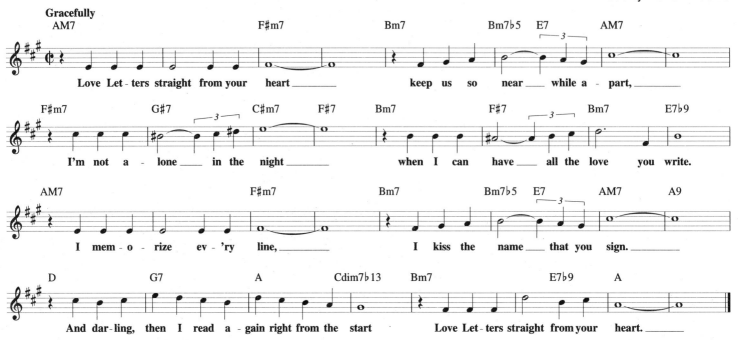

LOVE IS THE SWEETEST THING

Words and Music by
RAY NOBLE

A LOVELY WAY TO SPEND AN EVENING

Words by HAROLD ADAMSON
Music by JIMMY McHUGH

LOVE ME OR LEAVE ME
from LOVE ME OR LEAVE ME

Lyrics by GUS KAHN
Music by WALTER DONALDSON

LOVER
from the Paramount Picture LOVE ME TONIGHT

Words by LORENZ HART
Music by RICHARD RODGERS

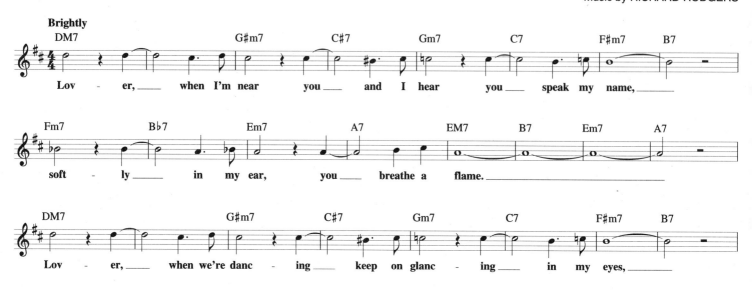

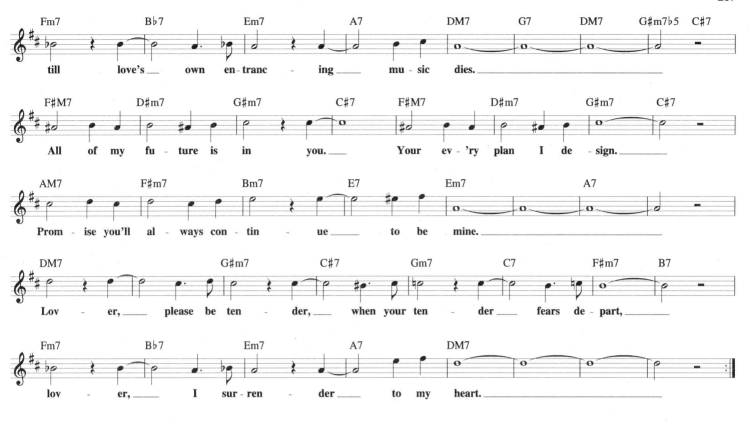

LIGIA

Words and Music by
ANTONIO CARLOS JOBIM

LAST RESORT

Written by RON CARTER

LATE LAMENT

By PAUL DESMOND

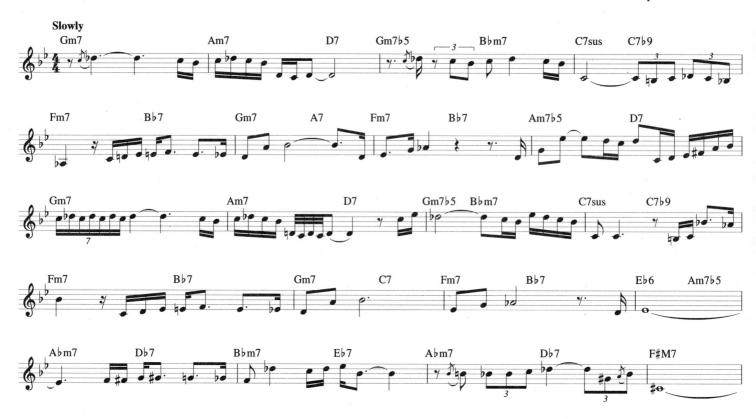

LIVIN'

Written by KEVIN EUBANKS

LONELY GIRL
from the Paramount Motion Picture HARLOW

Words by RAY EVANS and JAY LIVINGSTON
Music by NEAL HEFTI

LADY BIRD

By TADD DAMERON

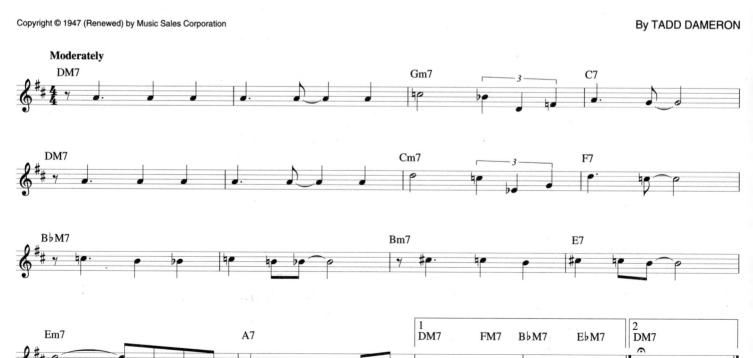

LAMENT

By J.J. JOHNSON

LAURIE

Music by BILL EVANS

LA FIESTA

By CHICK COREA

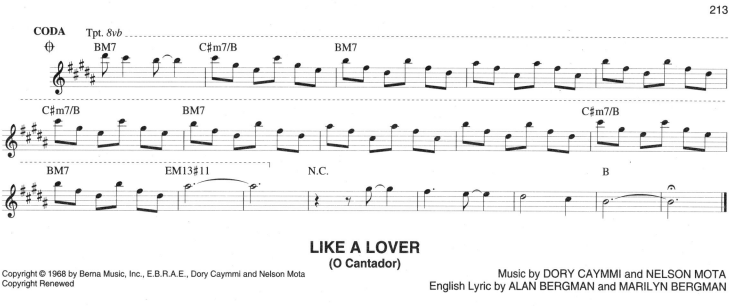

LIKE A LOVER
(O Cantador)

Music by DORY CAYMMI and NELSON MOTA
English Lyric by ALAN BERGMAN and MARILYN BERGMAN

LAZY RIVER

Words and Music by HOAGY CARMICHAEL
and SIDNEY ARODIN

LISTEN HERE

Words and Music by
DAVE FRISHBERG

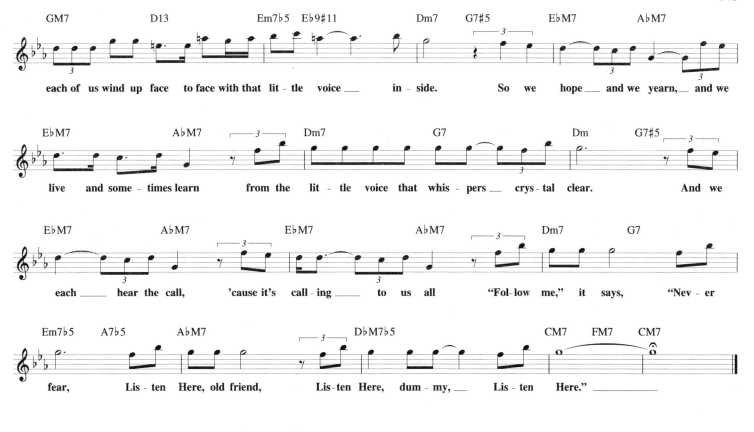

each of us wind up face to face with that lit-tle voice ___ in-side.   So we hope ___ and we yearn,___ and we

live and some-times learn   from the lit-tle voice that whis-pers ___ crys-tal clear.   And we

each ___ hear the call,   'cause it's call-ing ___ to us all   "Fol-low me," it says,   "Nev-er

fear,   Lis-ten Here, old friend,   Lis-ten Here, dum-my, ___   Lis-ten Here." _____

LEMON DROP

Copyright © 1950 (Renewed 1987) Jazz Editions

Composed by
GEORGE WALLINGTON

Moderately fast

LITTLE SHOES

By MIKE STERN

LITTLE SUNFLOWER

By FREDDIE HUBBARD

LOVE LIES

Words and Music by CARL SIGMAN,
RALPH FREED and JOSEPH MEYER

LITTLE WALTZ

Written by RON CARTER

LYDIA

By JACK DeJOHNETTE

LOVE YOU MADLY

By Duke Ellington

MISSION: IMPOSSIBLE THEME

from the Paramount Television Series MISSION: IMPOSSIBLE

by LALO SCHIFRIN

MAKE BELIEVE
from SHOW BOAT

Lyrics by OSCAR HAMMERSTEIN II
Music by JEROME KERN

MAKIN' WHOOPEE!
from WHOOPEE!

Lyrics by GUS KAHN
Music by WALTER DONALDSON

MAKE A LIST
(Make a Wish)

Written by ART PEPPER

MANTECA

By DIZZY GILLESPIE, WALTER "GIL" FULLER
and LUCIANO POZO GONZALES

ME AND MY BABY

Words and Music by
HORACE SILVER

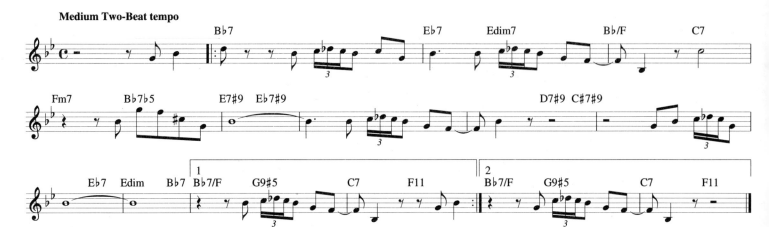

Intro (Male)
I've been puttin' it together day by day.
I've finally worked it out.

Chorus (Male)
I got plans,
I really got some plans
For Me And My Baby.
A brand new Cadillac.
And I don't mean maybe.
They won't take it back
From Me And My Baby.

She's my spouse.
I'm gonna buy a house
For Me And My Baby.
Way out in Malibu.
And I don't mean maybe.
Plenty money too.
For Me And My Baby.

If I work
And stash a bit away
For Me And My Baby.
Now there will come a day
And I don't mean maybe.
No more dues to pay.
For Me And My Baby.

SHOUT CHORUS (Male & Female)
(To be sung twice)
We're strivin' to live the good life.
There's nothin' that we can't do.
We've got our plans in full view.
We're gonna come in on cue.
We're not about to sub-due.
We're gonna see it on through.

TAG ENDING (Male & Female)
We will get to crackin'
So there's nothin' lackin'.
We will start attackin'
Send out doubts a-packin'.
We will keep on backin'
All the plans that we have
Carefully worked out
For Me And My Baby.

FOLLOWED BY CHORUS (Female)
He's my man
I'm doin' all I can
For me and my baby.
He sure can count on me.
And I don't mean maybe.
Perfect harmony
For Me And My Baby.

There's no doubt
That things will all work out
For Me And My Baby.
Our dreams will all come true.
And I don't mean maybe.
No more feelin' blue
For Me And My Baby.

Wait and see.
There'll be a family.
For Me And My Baby.
We've planned it carefully.
And I don't mean maybe.
Blessings they will be
For Me And My Baby.

*AFTER SHOUT CHORUS GO BACK
TO INTRO AND SING THROUGH
THEN TAKE TAG ENDING OUT*

MONA LISA
from the Paramount Picture CAPTAIN CAREY, U.S.A.

Words and Music by JAY LIVINGSTON
and RAY EVANS

dreams have been brought to your door-step. They just lie there, and they die there. Are you
warm, are you real, Mo-na Li-sa, or just a cold and lone-ly love-ly work of art? Mo-na art?

MAPUTO

By MARCUS MILLER

MOROCCO

By RUSS FREEMAN

CODA

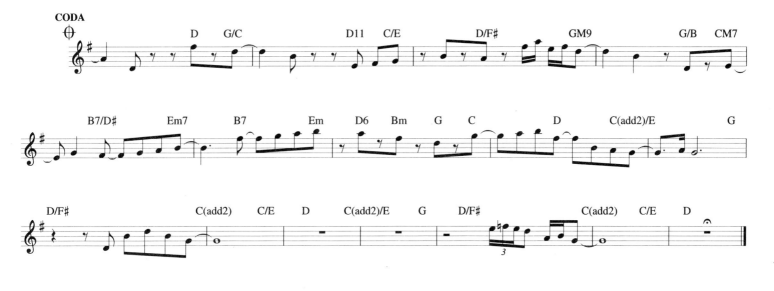

MOOD INDIGO
from SOPHISTICATED LADIES

Words and Music by DUKE ELLINGTON,
IRVING MILLS and ALBANY BIGARD

Moderately slow

226

DAYS OF WINE AND ROSES

Lyric by JOHNNY MERCER
Music by HENRY MANCINI

MR. BIG FALLS HIS J.G. HAND

Written by ART PEPPER

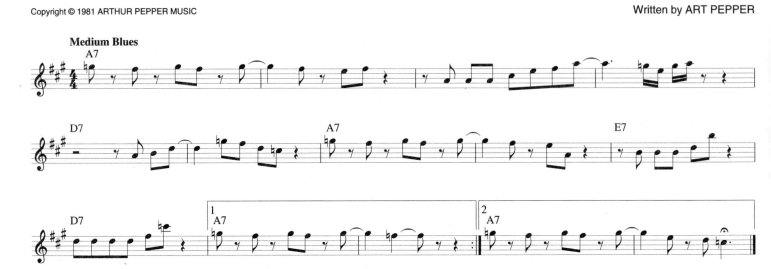

MY ATTORNEY BERNIE

Words and Music by
DAVE FRISHBERG

MR. GONE

Music by JOSEF ZAWINUL

MAIDEN VOYAGE

Music by HERBIE HANCOCK

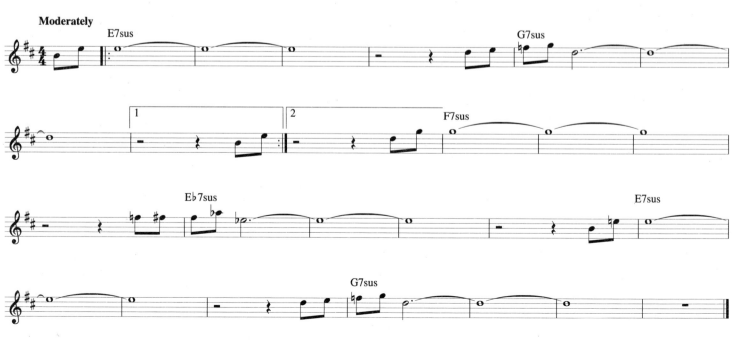

(I'm Afraid)
THE MASQUERADE IS OVER

Words by HERB MAGIDSON
Music by ALLIE WRUBEL

MORNIN'

Words and Music by AL JARREAU,
JAY GRAYDON and DAVID FOSTER

MOMENT'S NOTICE

By JOHN COLTRANE

MAMBO A LA SAVOY

Music and Lyric by WALTER "GIL" FULLER
Spanish Lyric by FRANK GRILLO (MACHITO)

Moderately

Here's the lat-est dance cre-a-tion, it's not a fad but a real sen-sa-tion; Lat-ins do it, you can do it too.

It was start-ed by a La-tin who brought the dance to all Man-hat-tan, and he called it Mam-bo A La Sa-voy.

When the band plays clav-es and rhy-thm, you start danc-ing by hyp-no-tism.

And you feel a new sen-sa-tion, it's the mam-bo with syn-co-pation. If you want some eas-y les-sons, just ask a Lat-in from Man-hat-tan and he'll teach you to Mam-bo A La Sa-voy.

MAS QUE NADA

Words and Music by
JORGE BEN

LAURA

Lyric by JOHNNY MERCER
Music by DAVID RAKSIN

MANOIR DE MES REVES
(Django's Castle)

By DJANGO REINHARDT

MIMOSA

By GEORGE BENSON

MANDY MAKE UP YOUR MIND

Words and Music by GRANT CLARKE,
ROY TURK, GEORGE MEYER and ARTHUR JOHNSTON

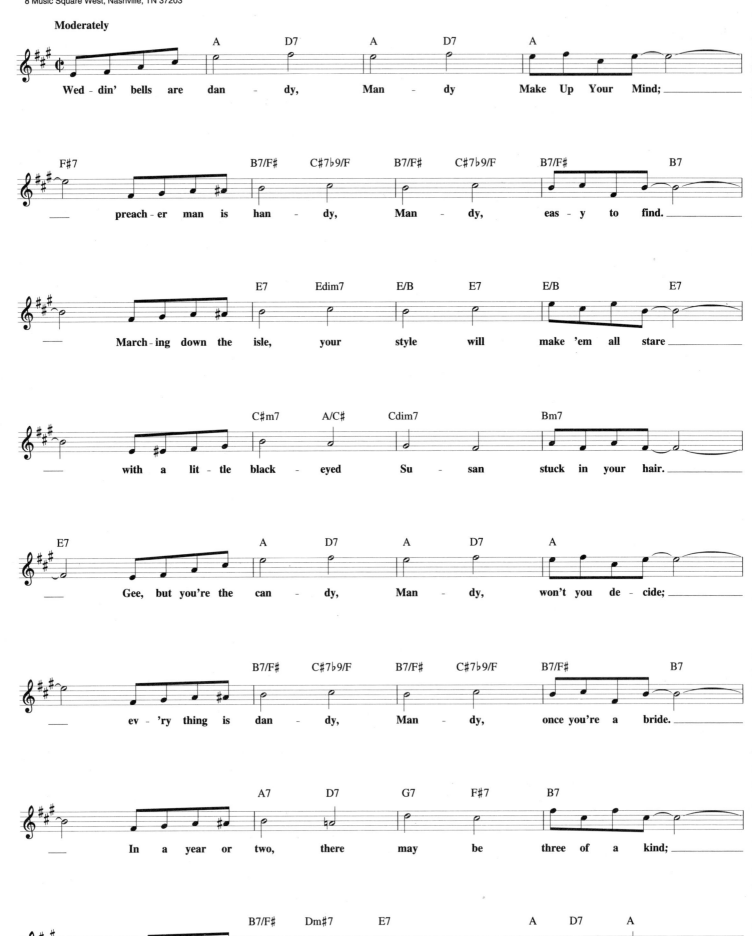

MR. LUCKY

Lyrics by JAY LIVINGSTON and RAY EVANS
Music by HENRY MANCINI

MR. JELLY-LORD

By FERDINAND "JELLY ROLL" MORTON

MR. WONDERFUL

Words and Music by JERRY BOCK,
LARRY HOLOFCENER and GEORGE DAVID WEISS

THE MOOCH

By DUKE ELLINGTON
and IRVING MILLS

MOON RIVER
from the Paramount Picture BREAKFAST AT TIFFANY'S

Words by JOHNNY MERCER
Music by HENRY MANCINI

MACK THE KNIFE
from THE THREEPENNY OPERA

Music by KURT WEILL
English Words by MARC BLITZSTEIN
Original German Words by BERT BRECHT

MORE I CANNOT WISH YOU
from GUYS AND DOLLS

By FRANK LOESSER

MOON OVER MIAMI

Lyric by EDGAR LESLIE
Music by JOE BURKE

MOONLIGHT BECOMES YOU
from the Paramount Picture ROAD TO MOROCCO

Words by JOHNNY BURKE
Music by JAMES VAN HEUSEN

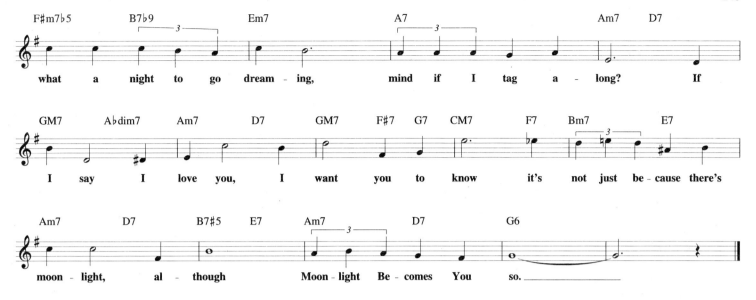

(There Ought to Be A)
MOONLIGHT SAVING TIME

Lyric and Music by IRVING KAHAL
and HARRY RICHMAN

246

LULLABY OF BIRDLAND

Words by GEORGE DAVID WEISS
Music by GEORGE SHEARING

MORNING DANCE

By JAY BECKENSTEIN

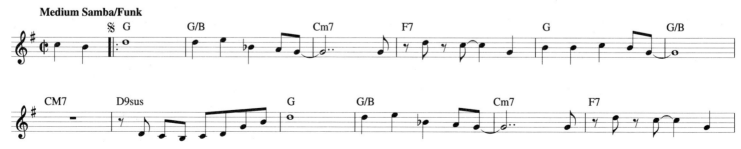

MY BABY JUST CARES FOR ME

Lyrics by GUS KAHN
Music by WALTER DONALDSON

MOST GENTLEMEN DON'T LIKE LOVE
from LEAVE IT TO ME!

Words and Music by
COLE PORTER

Additional Lyrics

2. Most Gentlemen Don't Like Love,
They just like to kick it around,
Most Gentlemen Don't Like Love,
'Cause most gentlemen can't be profound.
So just remember when you get that glance,
A romp and a quickie
Is all little Dickie means
When he mentions romance,
For Most Gentlemen Don't Like Love,
They just like to kick it around.

3. Most Gentlemen Don't Like Love,
They just like to kick it around,
Most Gentlemen Don't Like Love,
'Cause most gentlemen can't be profound.
In ev'ry land, children, they're all the same,
A pounce in the clover
And then when it's over
"So long and what is your name?"
'Cause Most Gentlemen Don't Like Love,
They just like to kick it around.

4. Most Gentlemen Don't Like Love,
They just like to kick it around,
Most Gentlemen Don't Like Love,
'Cause most gentlemen can't be profound.
So if your boy friend, some fine night,
Should say he'll love you forever
And part from you never,
Just push him out of the hay, (way)
'Cause Most Gentlemen Don't Like Love,
They just like to kick it around.

MY HEART STOOD STILL

Words by LORENZ HART
Music by RICHARD RODGERS

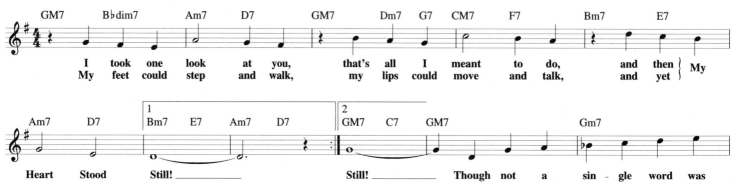

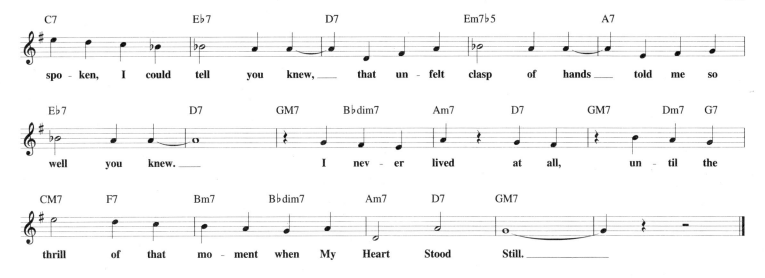

MOUNTAIN GREENERY
from the Broadway Musical THE GARRICK GAIETIES

Words by LORENZ HART
Music by RICHARD RODGERS

MY GIRL

Words and Music by WILLIAM "SMOKEY" ROBINSON
and RONALD WHITE

MY OLD FLAME
from the Paramount Picture BELLE OF THE NINETIES

Words and Music by ARTHUR JOHNSTON
and SAM COSLOW

MY SILENT LOVE

Words by EDWARD HEYMAN
Music by DANA SUESSE

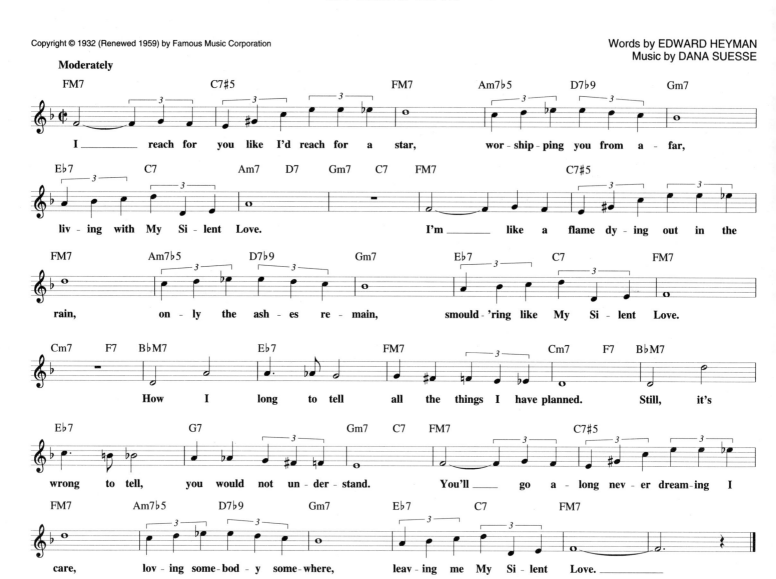

I _____ reach for you like I'd reach for a star, wor-ship-ping you from a-far, liv-ing with My Si-lent Love. I _____ like a flame dy-ing out in the rain, on-ly the ash-es re-main, smould-'ring like My Si-lent Love. How I long to tell all the things I have planned. Still, it's wrong to tell, you would not un-der-stand. You'll _____ go a-long nev-er dream-ing I care, lov-ing some-bod-y some-where, leav-ing me My Si-lent Love. _____

MY IDEAL

Words by LEO ROBIN
Music by RICHARD A. WHITING
and NEWELL CHASE

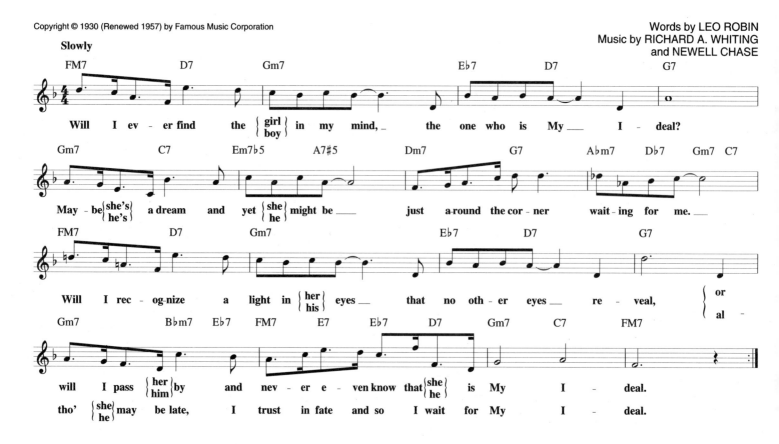

Will I ev-er find the {girl/boy} in my mind, _ the one who is My _ I-deal? May-be {she's/he's} a dream and yet {she/he} might be _____ just a-round the cor-ner wait-ing for me. _ Will I rec-og-nize a light in {her/his} eyes _ that no oth-er eyes _ re-veal, {or al-/will} I pass {her/him} by and nev-er e-ven know that {she/he} is My I-deal.
tho' {she/he} may be late, I trust in fate and so I wait for My I-deal.

NAIMA
(Niema)

By JOHN COLTRANE

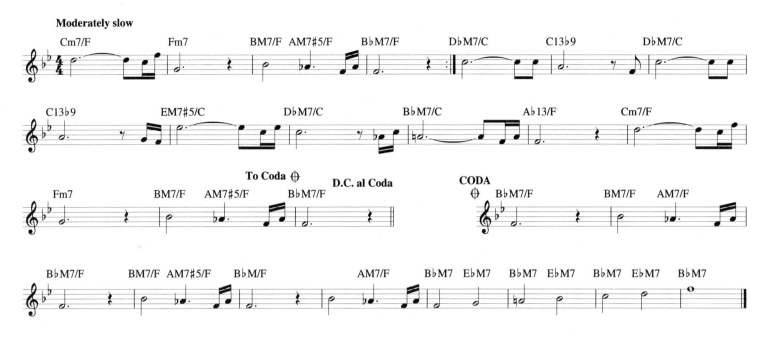

NATURE BOY

Words and Music by
EDEN AHBEZ

THE NEARNESS OF YOU
from the Paramount Picture ROMANCE IN THE DARK

Words by NED WASHINGTON
Music by HOAGY CARMICHAEL

NEARLY

Written by RON CARTER

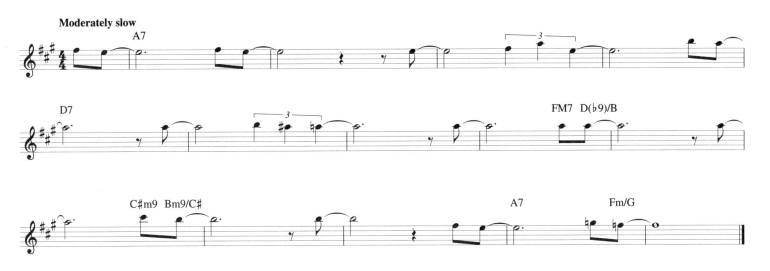

NEVER LET ME GO
from the Paramount Picture THE SCARLET HOUR

Words and Music by JAY LIVINGSTON
and RAY EVANS

NEW ORLEANS BLUES

By FERDINAND "JELLY ROLL" MORTON

YOU GOTTA PAY THE BAND

Words and Music by
ABBEY LINCOLN

THE NEXT TIME IT HAPPENS
from PIPE DREAM

Lyrics by OSCAR HAMMERSTEIN II
Music by RICHARD RODGERS

The Next Time It Hap-pens ___ I'll be wise e-nough to know ___ not to trust my eye-sight when my eyes be-gin to glow. ___ The next time I'm in love ___ with an-y-one like you, ___ my heart will sing no love song till I know the words are true. ___ "The Next Time It Hap-pens," ___ what a fool-ish thing to say! ___ Who ex-pects a mi-ra-cle to hap-pen ev-'ry day? ___ It is-n't in the cards ___ as far as I can see ___ that a thing so beau-ti-ful and won-der-ful could hap-pen more than once ___ to me. ___ me. ___

NIGHT TRAIN

Words by OSCAR WASHINGTON
and LEWIS C. SIMPKINS
Music by JIMMY FORREST

NICE PANTS

By BENNY GREEN

THE NIGHT HAS A THOUSAND EYES
Theme from the Paramount Picture THE NIGHT HAS A THOUSAND EYES

Words by BUDDY BERNIER
Music by JERRY BRAININ

NOBODY KNOWS YOU WHEN YOU'RE DOWN AND OUT

Words and Music by
JIMMIE COX

NOBODY'S HEART
from BY JUPITER

Words by LORENZ HART
Music by RICHARD RODGERS

NORWEGIAN WOOD
(This Bird Has Flown)

Words and Music by JOHN LENNON
and PAUL McCARTNEY

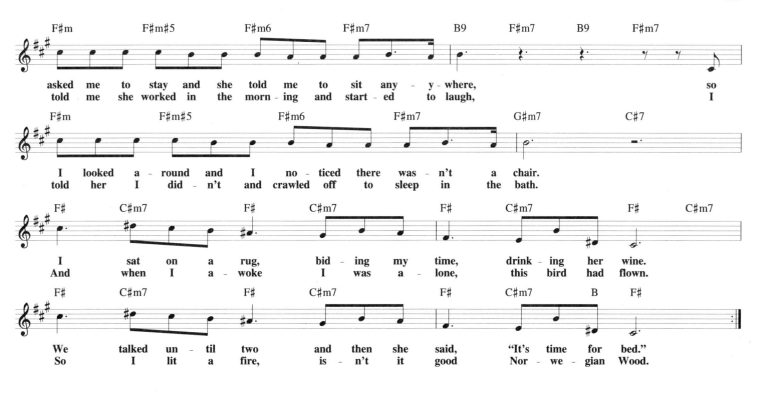

asked me to stay and she told me to sit any -- y - where,   so
told me she worked in the morn - ing and start - ed to laugh,   I

I looked a - round and I no - ticed there was -- n't a chair.
told her I did -- n't and crawled off to sleep in the bath.

I sat on a rug, bid - ing my time, drink - ing her wine.
And when I a - woke I was a - lone, this bird had flown.

We talked un - til two and then she said, "It's time for bed."
So I lit a fire, is -- n't it good Nor - we - gian Wood.

NOW IT CAN BE TOLD
from ALEXANDER'S RAGTIME BAND

Words and Music by
IRVING BERLIN

Slowly

Now It Can Be Told, _____ told in all its glo - ry. _____ Now that we have met, the

world may know the sen - ti - men - tal sto - ry. _____ The great - est ro - mance they

ev - er knew _____ is wait - ing to _____ un - fold. _____

Now It Can Be Told _____ as an in - spi - ra - tion. _____

Ev - 'ry oth - er tale of "Boy meets Girl" is just an im - i - ta - tion. _____

The great love sto - ry has nev - er been told be - fore, but now, _____

Now It Can Be Told. _____   Told. _____

NUAGES

By DJANGO REINHARDT
and JACQUES LARUE

O MORRO NÃO TEM VEZ

(Favela)
(Somewhere in the Hills)

Words and Music by ANTONIO CARLOS JOBIM
and VINICIUS DE MORAES

OFF MINOR

By THELONIOUS MONK

ON BROADWAY

Words and Music by BARRY MANN, CYNTHIA WEIL,
MIKE STOLLER and JERRY LEIBER

ONCE I LOVED
(Amor Em Paz)
(Love in Peace)

Music by ANTONIO CARLOS JOBIM
Portuguese Lyrics by VINICIUS DE MORAES
English Lyrics by RAY GILBERT

ONE FINGER SNAP

By HERBIE HANCOCK

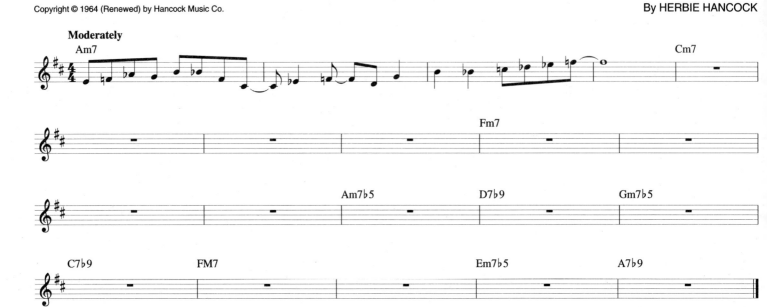

ONE FOR MY BABY
(And One More for the Road)
from the Motion Picture THE SKY'S THE LIMIT

Lyric by JOHNNY MERCER
Music by HAROLD ARLEN

ON GREEN DOLPHIN STREET

Lyrics by NED WASHINGTON
Music by BRONISLAU KAPER

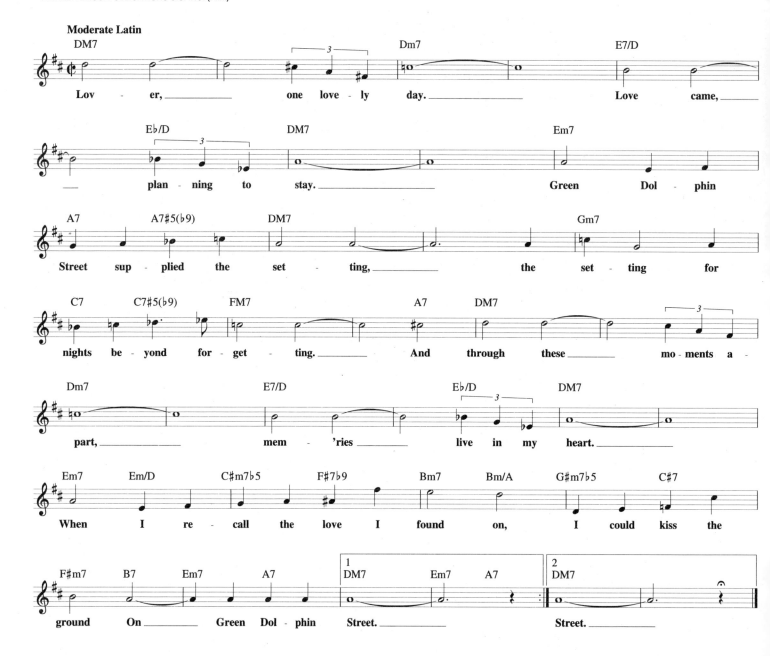

ON THE BORDER

By ERNIE WATTS

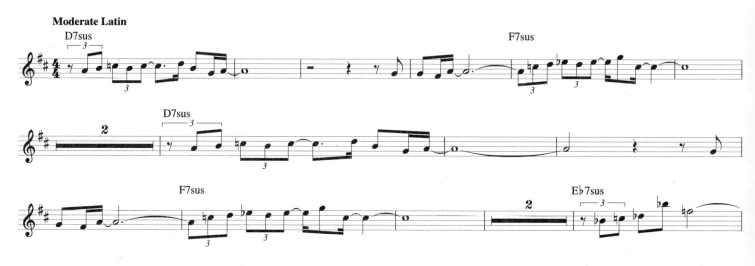

THE ONE I LOVE
(Belongs to Somebody Else)

Words by GUS KAHN
Music by ISHAM JONES

ORIGINAL RAYS

By MICHAEL BRECKER,
DON GROLNICK and MICHAEL STERN

PASSION DANCE

By McCOY TYNER

OUT OF NOWHERE
from the Paramount Picture DUDE RANCH

Words by EDWARD HEYMAN
Music by JOHNNY GREEN

Moderately

AM7 · Cm7 · F7 · AM7

You came to me _____ from Out Of No - where, _____ you took my heart _____

C#m7 · F#7 · Bm7 · Em7b5 · F#7

_____ and found it free. _____ Won - der - ful dreams, _ won - der - ful schemes _ from

Bm7 · F7 · Bm7

no - where made ev - 'ry hour sweet as a flow - er for me. _____

E7 · AM7 · Cm7 · F7

_____ If you should go _____ back to your no - where, _____

AM7 · C#m7 · F#7

leav - ing me with _____ a mem - o - ry, _____

Bm7 · C#m7b5 · F#7 · Bm7 · G7#11

I'll al - ways wait _____ for your re - turn Out Of No - where;

C#m7 · C · Bm7 · E7 · AM7

hop - ing you'll bring your love to me. _____

PARKING LOT BLUES

By RAY BROWN

Moderately

A13 · E7#9 A13 · C#7

D9 · A13 G#13 G13/C# F#7#9 · Bm7

A13 · E7#9 |1 A13 · E7#9 |2 A13

PASSION FLOWER

Words by MILTON RASKIN
Music by BILLY STRAYHORN

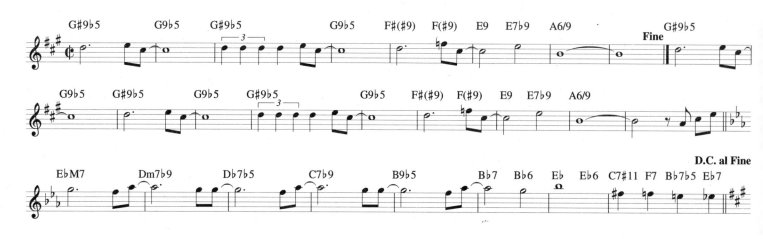

PEACE

Words and Music by
HORACE SILVER

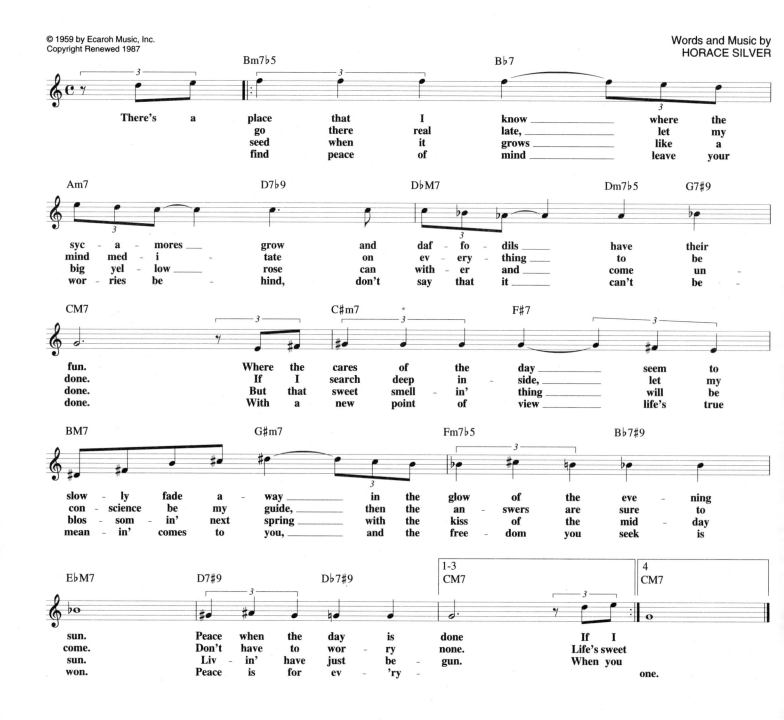

There's a place that I know _____ where the
go there I real late, _____ let my
seed when it grows _____ like a
find peace of mind _____ leave your

syc - a - mores _____ grow and daf - fo - dils _____ have their
mind med - i - tate on ev - ery - thing _____ to be
big yel - low _____ rose can with - er and _____ come un -
wor - ries be - hind, don't say that it _____ can't be

fun. Where the cares of the day _____ seem to
done. If I search deep in - side, _____ let my
done. But that sweet smell - in' thing _____ will be
done. With a new point of view _____ life's true

slow - ly fade a - way _____ in the glow of the eve - ning
con - science be my guide, _____ then the an - swers are sure to
blos - som - in' next spring _____ with the kiss of the mid - day
mean - in' comes to you, _____ and the free - dom you seek is

sun. Peace when the day is done. If I
come. Don't have to wor - ry none. Life's sweet
sun. Liv - in' have just be - gun. When you
won. Peace is for ev - 'ry - one.

Penthouse Serenade

Words and Music by WILL JASON
and VAL BURTON

Moderately

Pic - ture a pent-house way up in the sky, with hing - es on chim-neys for stars to go by, a

sweet slice of heav - en for just you and I when we're a - lone. From

all of so - ci - e - ty we'll stay a - loof, and live in pro - pri - e - ty there on the roof, two

heav - en - ly her-mits we will be in truth when we're a - lone. We'll see life's mad

pat - tern as we view old Man - hat - tan, then we can thank our

luck - y stars that we're liv - ing as we are. In our lit - tle pent-house, we'll

al - ways con - trive to keep love and ro - mance for - ev - er a - live, in view of the Hud-son just

o - ver the Drive, when we're a - lone. Just lone.

PEOPLE IN ME

Words and Music by
ABBEY LINCOLN

Additional Lyrics

2. I got some Chinese in me,
Some German in me,
I got some Japanese in me,
And blood from Vietnamese,

I got Some People In Me,
I Got Some People In Me,
I got the whole of Asianus
Turning in me,

3. I got some Jewish in me,
Some Arab in me,
I am Mexican rose,
I got some Russian in me,

I Got Some People In Me,
I Got some people in me,
I got the whole of Europaeus
Turning in me,

4. I got some lessons in me,
I got some learning in me,
I got whatever people know right now,
Inside of me,

I got some children in me,
I got some children in me,
I got the whole of Americanus
Turning in me,

5. I got some Guinee in me,
Some Ghana in me,
Some Zairewah blood,
I Got Some People In Me,

Dahomey in me,
Uganda in me,
Some Algerian blood,
I Got Some People In Me,

6. I got some French blood in me,
Sierra Leone in me,
Mozambique in me,
Some Egyptian blood,
I Got Some People In Me,

7. I Got Some People In Me,
I Got Some People In Me,
I got the whole wide world...
(he hit me - she hit me - he hit me -
you started it - take your hands off of me -
you must be crazy - na na na na na na)
...Turning in me.

PERFIDIA

Words and Music by
ALBERTO DOMINGUEZ

276

PERI'S SCOPE

TRO - © Copyright 1965 (Renewed 1993) and 1975 Folkways Music Publishers, Inc., New York, NY

Music by BILL EVANS

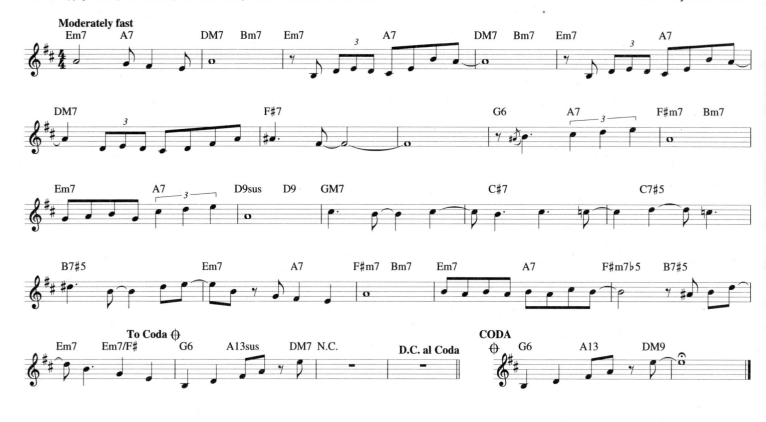

PHOEBE'S SAMBA

Copyright © 1990 Benny Green Music (BMI)

By BENNY GREEN

THE PLACE TO BE

By BENNY GREEN

PLEASE

from the Paramount Picture THE BIG BROADCAST OF 1933

Words by LEO ROBIN
Music by RALPH RAINGER

PLEASE SEND ME SOMEONE TO LOVE

Words and Music by
PERCY MAYFIELD

POTATO HEAD BLUES

By LOUIS ARMSTRONG

PURE IMAGINATION
from the film WILLY WONKA AND THE CHOCOLATE FACTORY

Words and Music by LESLIE BRICUSSE
and ANTHONY NEWLEY

POOR BUTTERFLY

Words by JOHN L. GOLDEN
Music by RAYMOND HUBBELL

PRELUDE TO A KISS

Words by IRVING GORDON and IRVING MILLS
Music by DUKE ELLINGTON

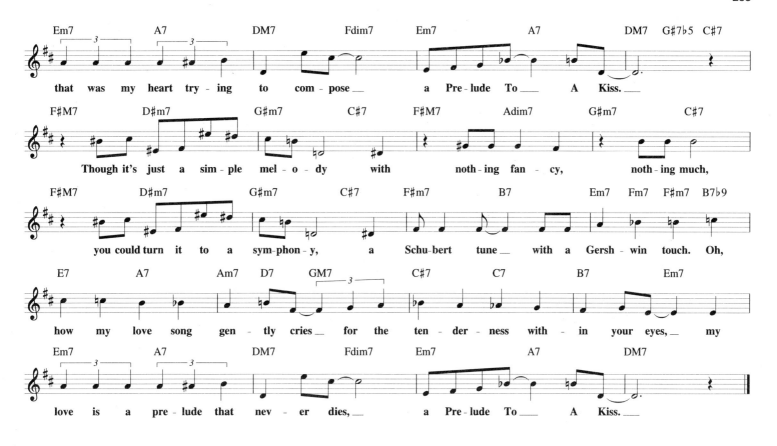

that was my heart try-ing to com-pose __ a Pre-lude To __ A Kiss. __

Though it's just a sim-ple mel-o-dy with noth-ing fan-cy, noth-ing much,

you could turn it to a sym-phon-y, a Schu-bert tune __ with a Gersh-win touch. Oh,

how my love song gen-tly cries __ for the ten-der-ness with-in your eyes, __ my

love is a pre-lude that nev-er dies, __ a Pre-lude To __ A Kiss. __

PURPLE ORCHIDS

By AL DI MEOLA

PRETEND

Words and Music by LEW DOUGLAS,
CLIFF PARMAN and FRANK LaVERE

P.S. I LOVE YOU

Words by JOHNNY MERCER
Music by GORDON JENKINS

Moderately

Dear, I thought I'd drop a line, the weath-er's cool, the folks are fine.

I'm in bed each night at nine, P. S. I Love You.

Yes-ter-day we had some rain, but all in all I can't com-plain.

Was it dust-y on the train? P. S. I Love You. Write to the Browns just as / I do my best to o-

soon as you're a-ble, ___ they came a-round to call. ___
bey all your wish-es, ___ I put a sign up Think! ___ But

I burned a hole in the din-ingroom ta-ble, ___ and let me see, I guess that's all. ___
I got-ta buy us a new set of dish-es, ___ or wash the ones, piled in the sink! _

Noth-ing else for me to say, and so I'll close, but by the way,
Noth-ing else to tell you dear, ex-cept each day seems like a year.

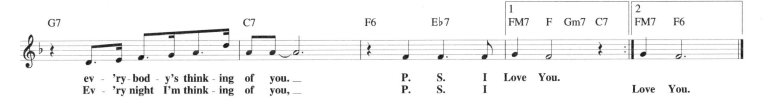

ev-'ry-bod-y's think-ing of you. ___ P. S. I Love You.
Ev-'ry night I'm think-ing of you, ___ P. S. I Love You.

THE RAINBOW CONNECTION
from THE MUPPET MOVIE

By PAUL WILLIAMS
and KENNETH L. ASCHER

RE: PERSON I KNEW

Music by BILL EVANS

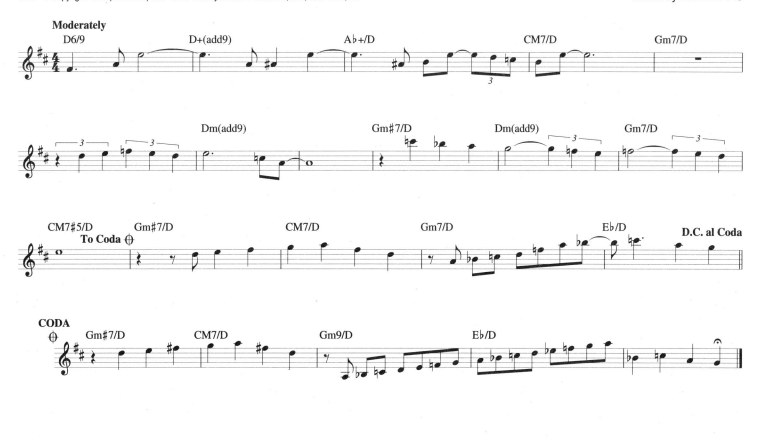

RED CLAY

By FREDDIE HUBBARD

A REMARK YOU MADE

Music by JOSEF ZAWINUL

REMIND ME

Words and Music by DOROTHY FIELDS
and JEROME KERN

REMEMBER

Words and Music by
IRVING BERLIN

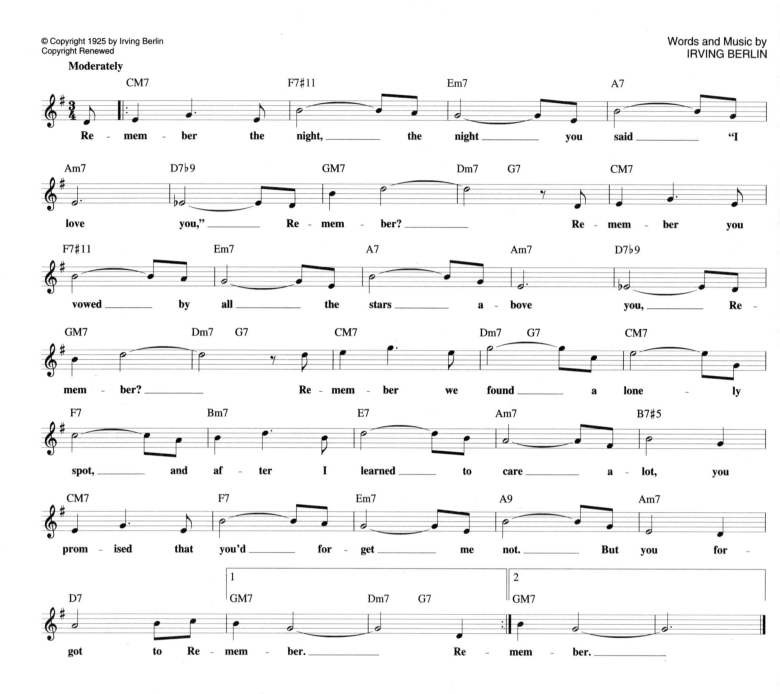

RESEMBLANCE

Written by EDDIE PALMIERI

RIDIN' HIGH
from RED, HOT AND BLUE!

Words and Music by
COLE PORTER

Moderately fast

Life's great, _ life's grand, _ fu - ture ___
Some - one _ I love, ___ mad for ___
ring bells, _ sing songs, _ blow horns.

all planned. _ No more _____ clouds in ___ the sky,
my love, _____ so long, _____ Jo - nah, _ good - bye.
beat gongs, _____ our love _____ nev - er _ will die.

how'm I _____ rid - in? ___ I'm Rid - in' High. ___
How'm I _____ rid - in? ___ I'm
How'm I _____   Rid - in' High. _

Float - ing ___ on a star - lit ceil - ing,

dot - ing ___ on the cards I'm deal - ing, gloat - ing, ___

be - cause I'm feel - ing so hap - hap - hap - py. I'm slap hap - py.

So rid - in? ___ I'm Rid - in' High. _____

RIFFTIDE

By COLEMAN HAWKINS
and STEVE GRAHAM

RITMO DE LA NOCHE

By AL DI MEOLA

RIGHT AS THE RAIN
from BLOOMER GIRL

Words by E.Y. Harburg
Music by HAROLD ARLEN

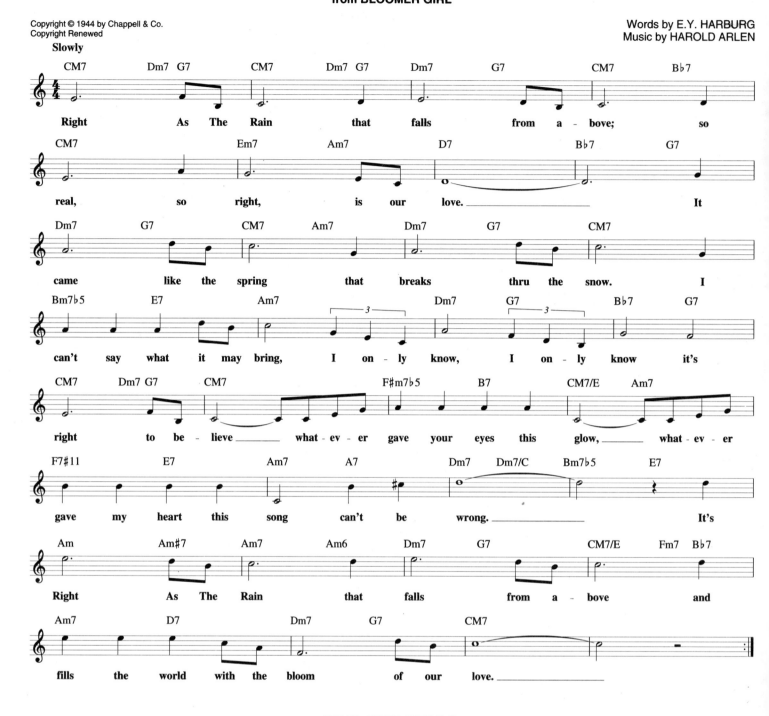

RING DEM BELLS

Words and Music by DUKE ELLINGTON
and IRVING MILLS

RIVERBOAT SHUFFLE

Words and Music by HOAGY CARMICHAEL, MITCHELL PARISH, IRVING MILLS and DICK VOYNOW

ROCKIN' IN RHYTHM

By DUKE ELLINGTON, IRVING MILLS
and HARRY CARNEY

ST. LOUIS BLUES
from BIRTH OF THE BLUES

Words and Music by
W. C. HANDY

ROCKER
(Rock Salt)

By GERRY MULLIGAN

SAMBA CANTINA

By PAUL DESMOND

SAY IT ISN'T SO

Words and Music by
IRVING BERLIN

Moderately

SEARCHING, FINDING

By JOHN PATITUCCI

SEGMENT

By CHARLIE PARKER

SEÑOR CARLOS

By McCOY TYNER

SEEMS LIKE OLD TIMES

Lyric and Music by JOHN JACOB LOEB
and CARMEN LOMBARDO

SERENGETI WALK
(Slippin' in the Back Door)

Words and Music by DAVE GRUSIN,
LOUIE JOHNSON and HARVEY MASON

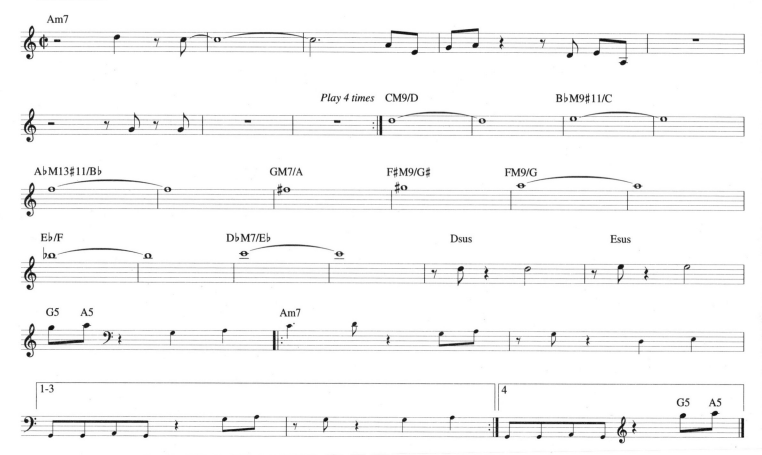

Señor Mouse

By CHICK COREA

SHAKER SONG

By JAY BECKENSTEIN

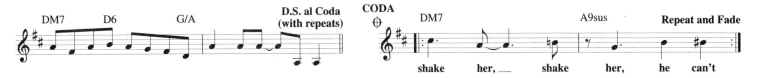

Additional Lyrics

2. The night hangs its head
   As the fool crawls into bed,
   Still his hungry heart begs to be fed
   All the words she once, that she said, that she said,
   So then he grabs his Chevrolet
   In one more attempt to get away
   But thoughts of all the crimes of passion lay,
   Lay in his way.

3. Romance falls like rain
   But all the motives are insane
   Every time that he plays the game he feels the pain,
   He feels the pain, who is to blame, who is to blame, who is to blame?
   And then he finds a joint that's jive,
   Guys are spinning girls like 45's,
   All of the live bait sinks for his lines,
   They are so high.

4. He knows he is beat
   As his heart puts on the heat,
   Run from the street that don't even fit his feet,
   Don't fit his feet, now he can see, now he can really see, now he can...
   Tell him where's a telephone,
   He can beg to let the fool come home,
   He tells her that his life's a drag alone,
   Can't be alone.

THE SHADOW OF YOUR SMILE
Love Theme from THE SANDPIPER

Lyric by PAUL FRANCIS WEBSTER
Music by JOHNNY MANDEL

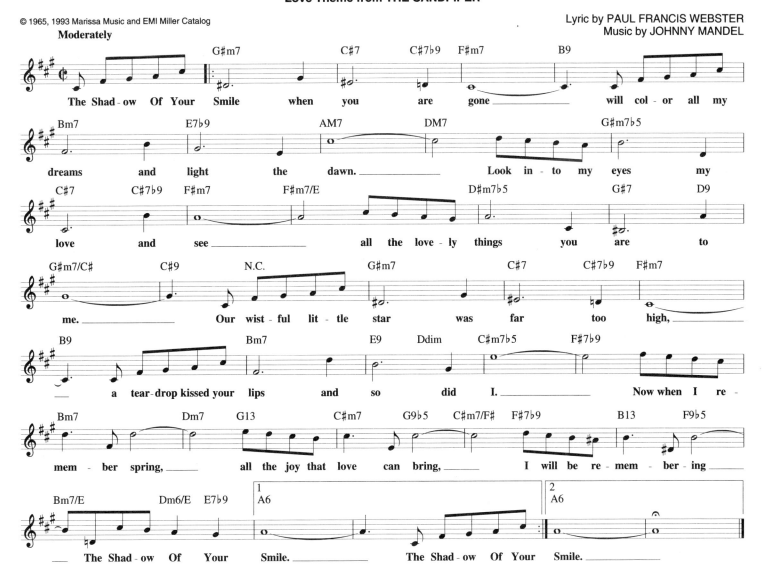

A SHIP WITHOUT A SAIL

Words by LORENZ HART
Music by RICHARD RODGERS

SILVER HOLLOW

By JACK DeJOHNETTE

SILHOUETTE

By KENNY G

SIMPLE SAMBA

By JAMES S. HALL

A SLEEPIN' BEE
from HOUSE OF FLOWERS

Lyric by TRUMAN CAPOTE and HAROLD ARLEN
Music by HAROLD ARLEN

THE SINGLE PETAL OF A ROSE
from QUEEN'S SUITE

By DUKE ELLINGTON

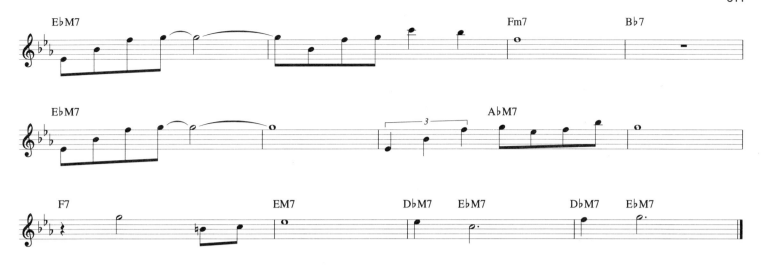

SIPPIN' AT BELLS

By MILES DAVIS

SO EASY

By TADD DAMERON
and ARTIE SHAW

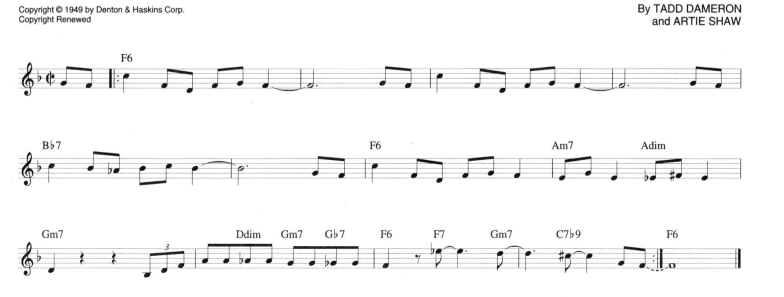

SLAUGHTER ON TENTH AVENUE
from ON YOUR TOES

By RICHARD RODGERS

SO IN LOVE
from KISS ME, KATE

Words and Music by
COLE PORTER

Moderately

Strange, dear, but true, dear. When I'm close to you, dear, the stars fill the sky, So In Love with you am I, E-ven with-out you, my arms fold a-bout you. You know, dar-ling, why, So In Love with you am I. In love with the right mys-te-ri-ous, the night when you first were there, in love with my joy de-lir-i-ous when I knew that you could care, So taunt me and hurt me, de-ceive me, de-sert me. I'm yours 'til I die, So In Love, So In Love, So In Love with you, my love am I.

SMILE FROM A STRANGER

By AL DI MEOLA

SO YOU SAY

By JOHN SCOFIELD

SOFT LIGHTS AND SWEET MUSIC
from the Stage Production FACE THE MUSIC

Words and Music by
IRVING BERLIN

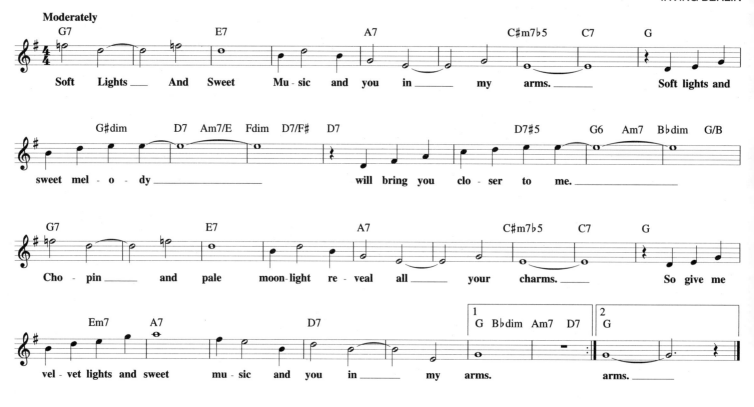

SOFTLY AS IN A MORNING SUNRISE
from THE NEW MOON

Lyric by OSCAR HAMMERSTEIN II
Music by SIGMUND ROMBERG

SOME SKUNK FUNK

By RANDY BRECKER

318

SOLEA

Written by GIL EVANS

Copyright © 1960 (Renewed 1988) BOPPER SPOCK SUNS MUSIC

SOMEBODY LOVES ME
from SHE LOVES ME

Copyright © 1924 Stephen Ballentine Music and Warner Bros. Inc.
Copyright Renewed
All Rights for Stephen Ballentine Music Administered by The Songwriters Guild Of America

Words by B.G. DeSYLVA and BALLARD MACDONALD
Music by GEORGE GERSHWIN
French Version by EMELIA RENAUD

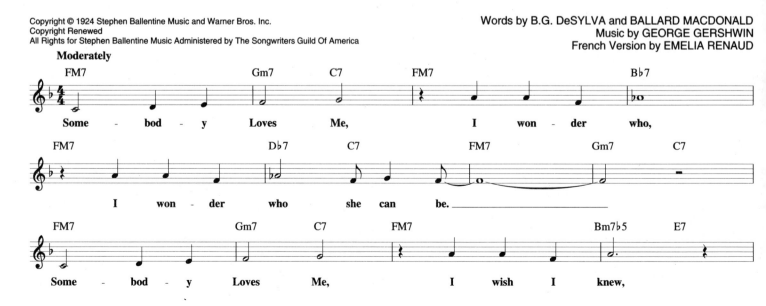

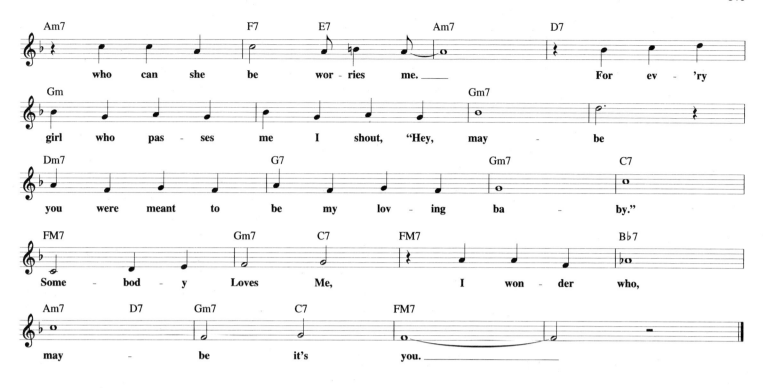

SOMETHING I DREAMED LAST NIGHT

Words and Music by SAMMY FAIN,
HERBERT MAGIDSON and JACK YELLEN

SOMEWHERE ALONG THE WAY

Words by SAMMY GALLOP
Music by KURT ADAMS

SONG FOR LORRAINE

By JAY BECKENSTEIN

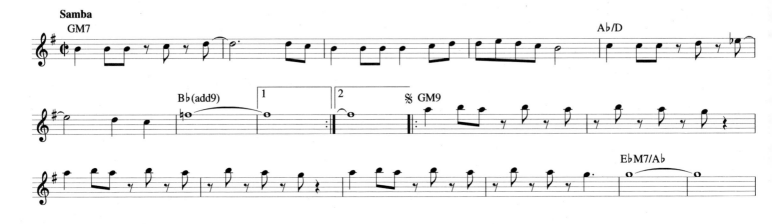

THE SONG IS ENDED
(But the Melody Lingers On)

Words and Music by
IRVING BERLIN

SONG FROM M*A*S*H
(Suicide Is Painless)

Words and Music by MIKE ALTMAN
and JOHNNY MANDEL

1. Through ear-ly morn-ing fog I see vis-ions of the things to be: the
2. - 6. (See additional lyrics)

pains that are with-held for me. I re-a-lize and I can see

that su-i-cide is pain-less, it brings on man-y chang-

-es, and I can take or leave it if I please. 2. I

And you can do the same thing if you

please.

Additional Lyrics

2. I try to find a way to make
   All our little joys relate
   Without that ever-present hate
   But now I know that it's too late.

3. The game of life is hard to play,
   I'm going to lose it anyway,
   The losing card I'll someday lay,
   So this is all I have to say.

4. The only way to win is cheat
   And lay it down before I'm beat,
   And to another give a seat,
   For that's the only painless feat.

5. The sword of time will pierce our skins,
   It doesn't hurt when it begins
   But as it works it's way on in,
   The pain grows stronger, watch it grin.

6. A brave man once requested me
   To answer questions that are key,
   Is it to be or not to be
   And I replied; "Oh, why ask me."

SONG FOR STRAYHORN

By GERRY MULLIGAN

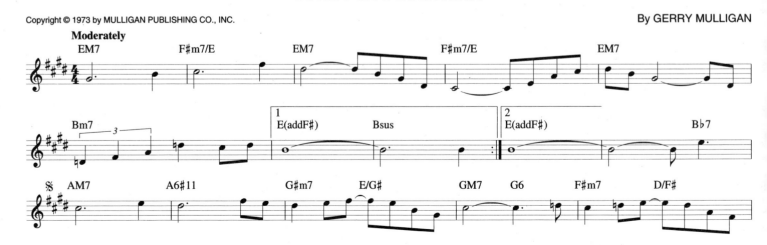

SONGBIRD

By KENNY G

STABLEMATES

By BENNY GOLSON

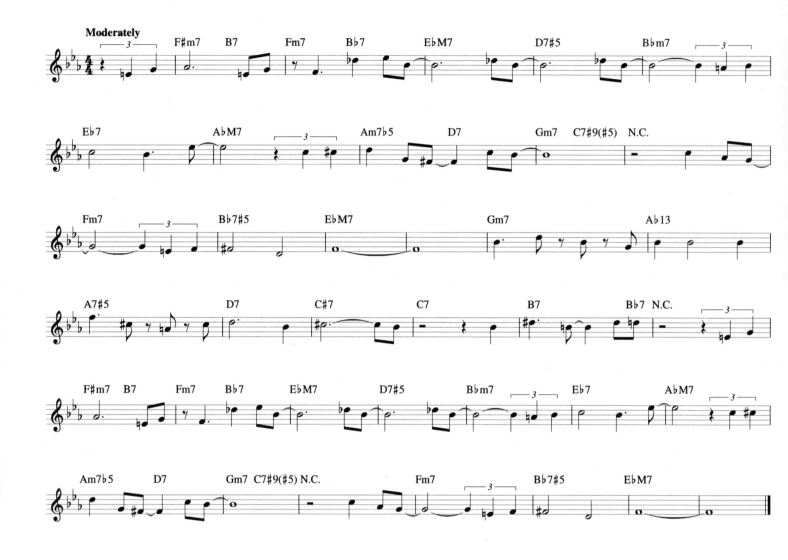

SOPHISTICATED LADY
from SOPHISTICATED LADIES

Words and Music by DUKE ELLINGTON,
IRVING MILLS and MITCHELL PARISH

STAIRWAY TO THE STARS

Words by MITCHELL PARISH
Music by MATT MALNECK and FRANK SIGNORELLI

SOMEONE TO LIGHT UP MY LIFE
(Se Todos Fossem Iguais a Voce)

English Lyric by GENE LEES
Original Text by VINICIUS DE MORAES
Music by ANTONIO CARLOS JOBIM

STARDREAMS

Words and Music by CHARLES SPIVAK,
SONNY BURKE and SYLVIA DEE

STELLA BY STARLIGHT
from the Paramount Picture THE UNINVITED

Words by NED WASHINGTON
Music by VICTOR YOUNG

STAR DUST

Words by MITCHELL PARISH
Music by HOAGY CARMICHAEL

STEPPIN' OUT WITH MY BABY

from the Motion Picture Irving Berlin's EASTER PARADE

Words and Music by
IRVING BERLIN

© Copyright 1947 by Irving Berlin
Copyright Renewed

STILL WARM

By JOHN SCOFIELD

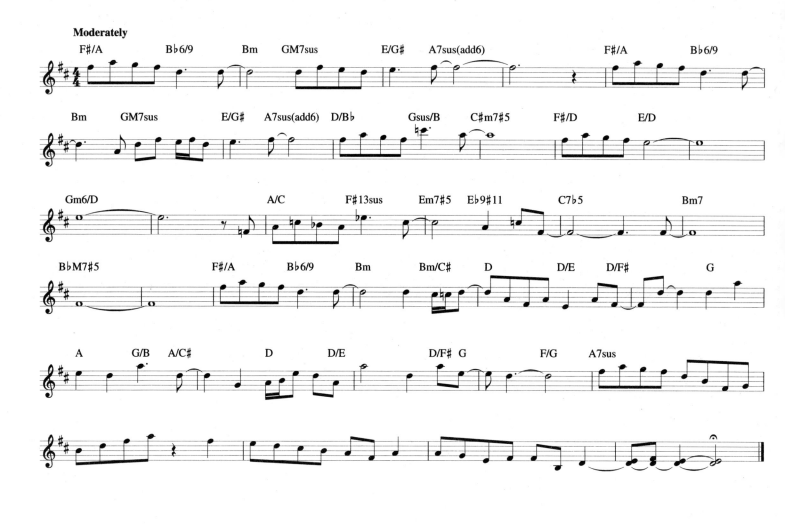

STOLEN MOMENTS

Words and Music by
OLIVER NELSON

STEREOPHONIC

By ERNEST B. WILKINS

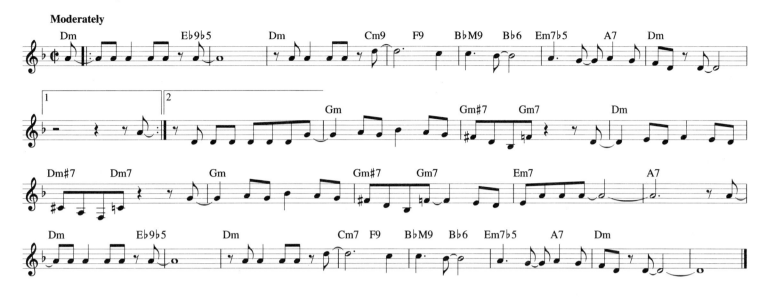

STORY OF MY FATHER

Words and Music by
ABBEY LINCOLN

Additional Lyrics

2. My father built us houses,
   And he kept his folks inside,
   His images were stolen,
   And his beauty was denied,

3. My brothers are unhappy,
   My sisters they are too,
   My mother prays for glory,
   And my father stands accused,

4. My father, yes my father,
   A brace and skillful man,
   He fed and served his people,
   With the magic of his hand,

5. My father, yes my father,
   His soul was sorely tried,
   'Cause his images were stolen,
   And his beauty was denied,

6. Sometimes the river's calling
   Sometimes the shadows fall,
   That's when he's like a mountain,
   Rising master over all,

7. This Story Of My Father,
   Is the one I tell and give,
   It's the power and the glory,
   Of the life I make and live,

8. My father has a kingdom,
   My father wears a crown,
   And he lives within the people,
   In the lives he handed down.

9. My father has a kingdom,
   My father wears a crown,
   And through the spirit of my mother, Lord,
   The crown was handed down.

STRAIGHT LIFE

Written by ART PEPPER

STRAPHANGIN'

By MICHAEL BRECKER

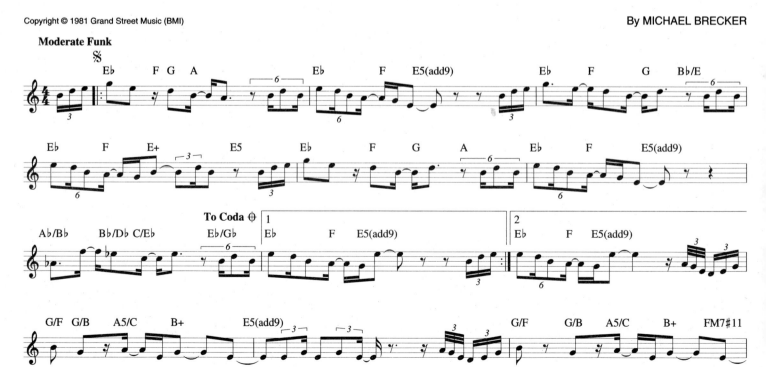

STROLLIN'

Words and Music by
HORACE SILVER

SUDDENLY IT'S SPRING
from the Paramount Motion Picture LADY IN THE DARK

Words by JOHNNY BURKE
Music by JAMES VAN HEUSEN

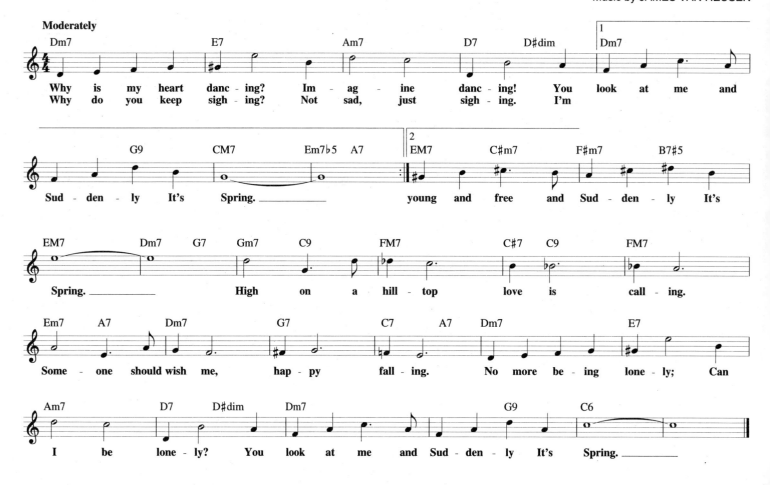

SUN

Written by KEVIN EUBANKS

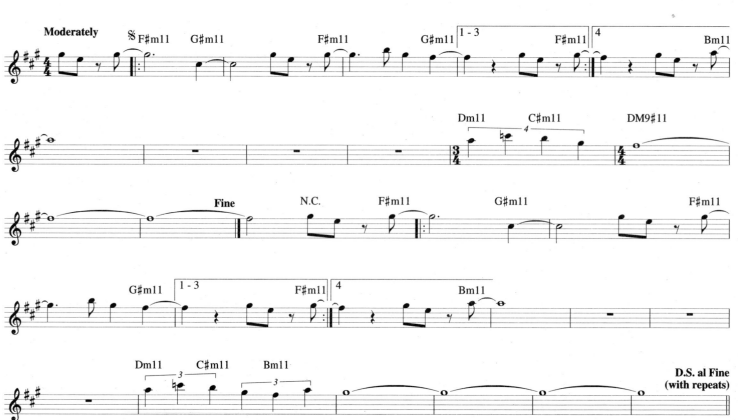

SWAY
(Quien Sera)

English Words and Music by NORMAN GIMBEL
Spanish Words by PABLO BELTRAN RUIZ

SUNDAY IN NEW YORK

By PORTIA NELSON

SURF RIDE

Written by ART PEPPER

TAKE A WALK

By MICHAEL BRECKER

SWING 41

By DJANGO REINHARDT

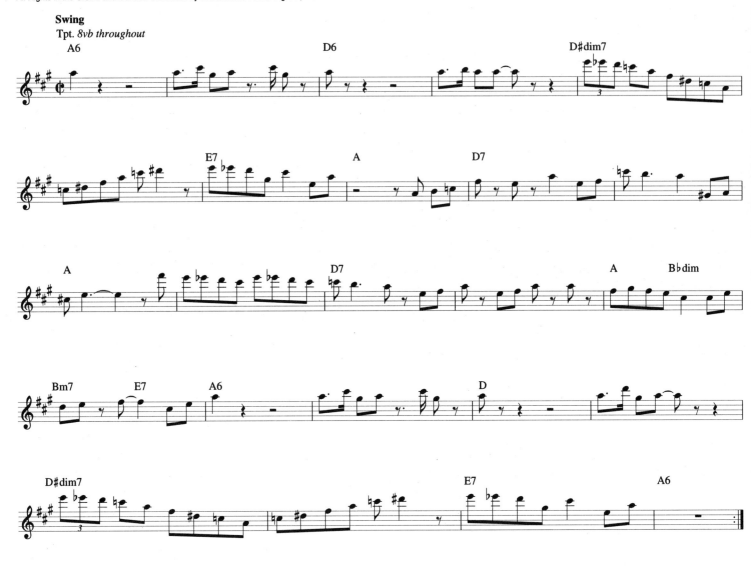

TANGERINE
from the Paramount Picture THE FLEET'S IN

Words by JOHNNY MERCER
Music by VICTOR SCHERTZINGER

TEACH ME TONIGHT

Words by SAMMY CAHN
Music by GENE DePAUL

TAKE FIVE

By PAUL DESMOND

TAKE TEN

By PAUL DESMOND

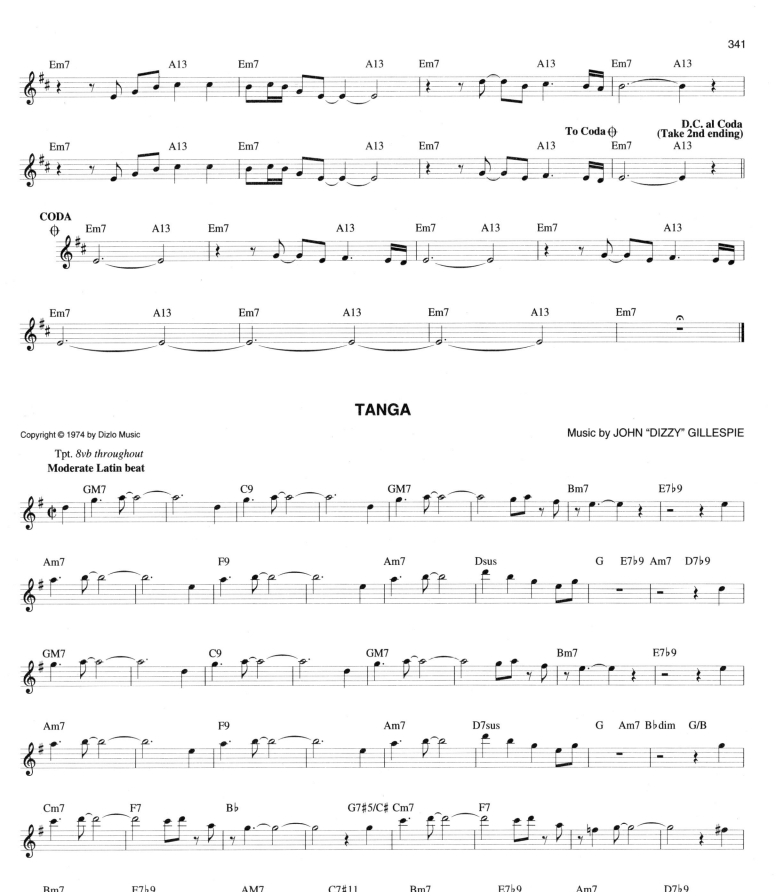

TANGA

Music by JOHN "DIZZY" GILLESPIE

Tpt. *8vb throughout*
Moderate Latin beat

TELL ME A BEDTIME STORY

By HERBIE HANCOCK

THERE'S A MINGUS AMONK US

By RANDY BRECKER

THINGS AIN'T WHAT THEY USED TO BE

By MERCER ELLINGTON

THANKS FOR THE MEMORY
from the Paramount Picture BIG BROADCAST OF 1938

Words and Music by LEO ROBIN
and RALPH RAINGER

THAT OLD BLACK MAGIC
from the Paramount Picture STAR SPANGLED RHYTHM

Words by JOHNNY MERCER
Music by HAROLD ARLEN

THAT'S RIGHT

By BENNY GREEN

THINGS TO COME

By DIZZY GILLESPIE and GIL FULLER

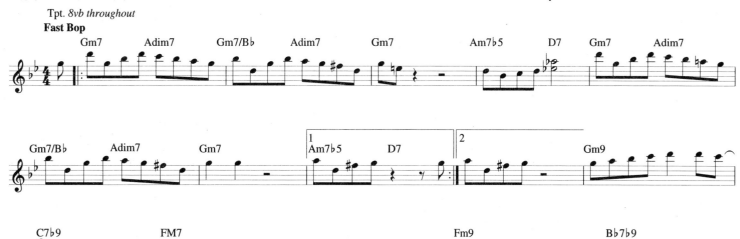
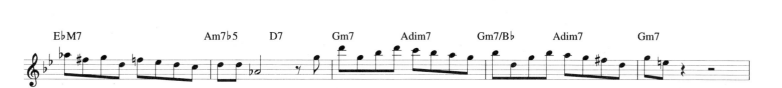

THE THIRD PLANE

Written by RON CARTER

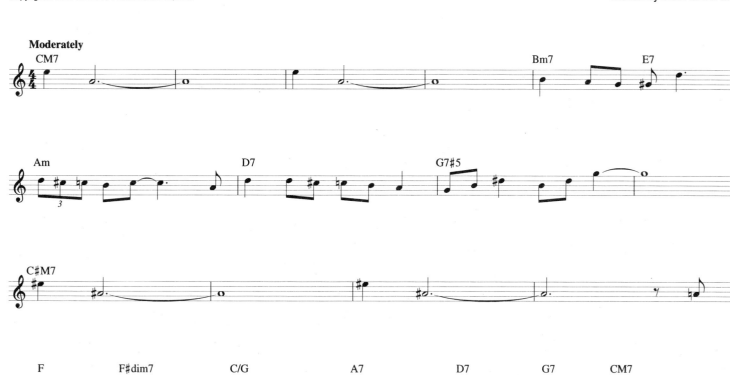

THIS IS ALL I ASK
(Beautiful Girls Walk a Little Slower)

Words and Music by
GORDON JENKINS

THIS YEAR'S KISSES
from the 20th Century Fox Motion Picture ON THE AVENUE

Words and Music by
IRVING BERLIN

THREE LITTLE WORDS
from the Motion Picture CHECK AND DOUBLE CHECK

Lyric by BERT KALMAR
Music by HARRY RUBY

THIS MASQUERADE

Words and Music by
LEON RUSSELL

TIME WAS

English Words by S.K. RUSSELL
Music by MIGUEL PRADO

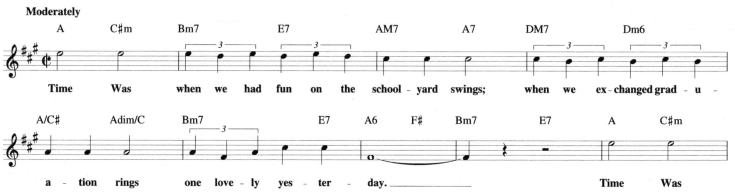

when we wrote love let - ters in the sand, or lin - gered o - ver our "cof - fee and,"

dream - ing the time a - way. _____ Pic - nics and hay - rides and

mid - win - ter sleigh rides and nev - er a - part. Hikes in the coun - try and

there's more than one tree on which I've a place in your heart.

Dar - ling, ev - 'ry to - mor - row will be com - plete, If all our mo - ments are

half as sweet as all our time was then. _____ then. _____

TILL THE CLOUDS ROLL BY
from OH BOY!

Words by P.G. WODEHOUSE
Music by JEROME KERN

Oh, the rain _____ comes a pit - ter, pat - ter, _____ and I'd like _____ to be safe in

bed. _____ Skies are weep - ing, _____ while the world is sleep - ing, _____ trou - ble heap - ing on

our head. _____ It is vain _____ to re - main and chat - ter, _____ and to

wait _____ for a clear - er sky. _____ Hel - ter skel - ter _____ I must fly for shel - ter _____

_____ Till The Clouds Roll By. Oh, the By. _____

TO EACH HIS OWN
from the Paramount Picture THE CONVERSATION

Words and Music by JAY LIVINGSTON
and RAY EVANS

Lyrics (line 1):
A rose _____ must re-main _____ with the sun _____ and the rain _____ or its love-ly prom-ise won't come true. _____ To Each His Own, To Each His Own, and my own is you. _____ What you. _____ If a flame is to grow there must be a glow, to o-pen each door there's a key. _____ I need you, I know I can't let you go, your touch means too much to me. _____ Two lips _____ must in-sist _____ on two more _____ to be kissed _____ or they'll nev-er know what love can do. _____ To Each His Own, I've found my own one and on-ly you.

Lyrics (line 2):
good _____ is a song _____ if the words just don't be-long _____ and a dream must be a dream for two. _____ No good a-lone, To Each His Own, for me there's

TOKU-DO

By BUSTER WILLIAMS

Too Close For Comfort
from the Musical MR. WONDERFUL

Words and Music by JERRY BOCK,
LARRY HOLOFCENER and GEORGE WEISS

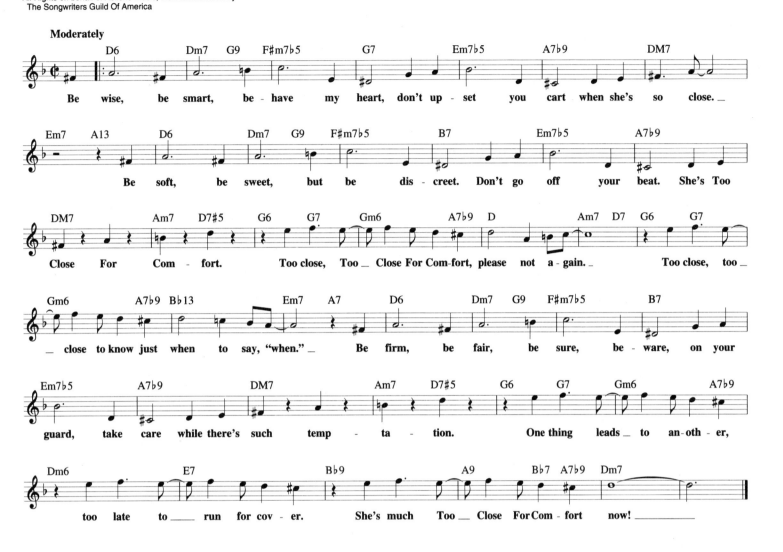

Topsy

Written by EDGAR BATTLE
and EDDIE DURHAM

TOURIST IN PARADISE

By RUSS FREEMAN

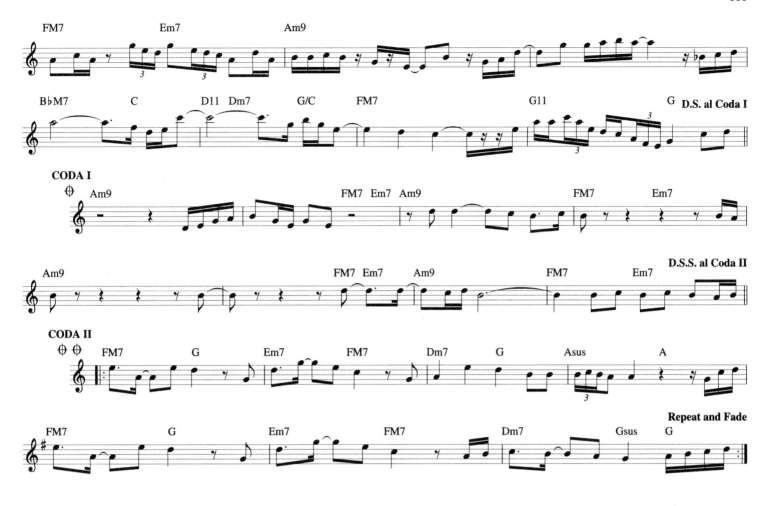

TWO OF A MIND

By PAUL DESMOND

TRISTE

By ANTONIO CARLOS JOBIM

ULTRAFOX

By DJANGO REINHARDT

THE VERY THOUGHT OF YOU

Words and Music by
RAY NOBLE

WALK DON'T RUN

Words and Music by
JOHNNY SMITH

Too Late Now

Words by ALAN JAY LERNER
Music by BURTON LANE

VISA

By CHARLIE PARKER

UNLESS IT'S YOU

Lyric by MORGAN AMES
Music by JOHNNY MANDEL

WATERMELON MAN

By HERBIE HANCOCK

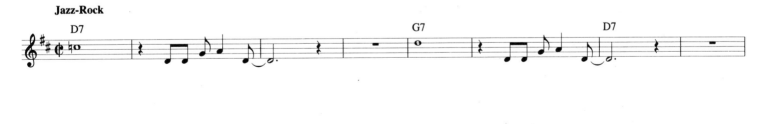

WALTZ NEW

By JAMES S. HALL

WAVE

Words and Music by
ANTONIO CARLOS JOBIM

The fun-da-men-tal lone - li-ness goes _ when-ev-er two can dream a dream to - geth - er. _

When I saw you first the time was half past three, _ when your eyes met

mine it was e - ter - ni - ty. _ By now we know the Wave is on its way to be. _

_ Just catch _ the Wave, _ don't be a - fraid _ of lov - ing me. _ The fun-da-men-tal lone -

- li - ness goes _ when-ev-er two can dream a dream to - geth - er. _

WE'LL BE TOGETHER AGAIN

Lyric by FRANKIE LAINE
Music by CARL FISCHER

Moderately slow

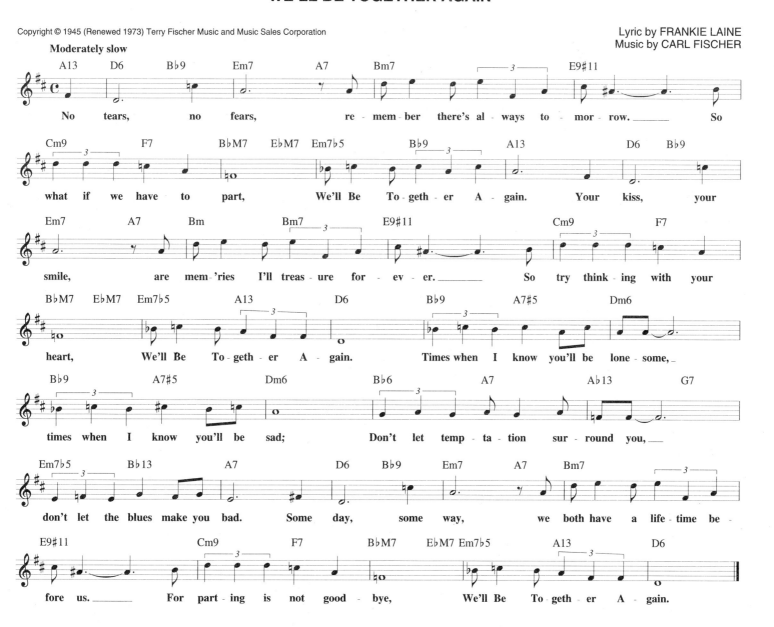

No tears, no fears, re - mem - ber there's al - ways to - mor - row. _ So

what if we have to part, We'll Be To - geth - er A - gain. Your kiss, your

smile, are mem - 'ries I'll treas - ure for - ev - er. _ So try think - ing with your

heart, We'll Be To - geth - er A - gain. Times when I know you'll be lone - some, _

times when I know you'll be sad; Don't let temp - ta - tion sur - round you, _

don't let the blues make you bad. Some day, some way, we both have a life - time be -

fore us. For part - ing is not good - bye, We'll Be To - geth - er A - gain.

WENDY

By PAUL DESMOND

WE THREE BLUES

By FRANK MORGAN

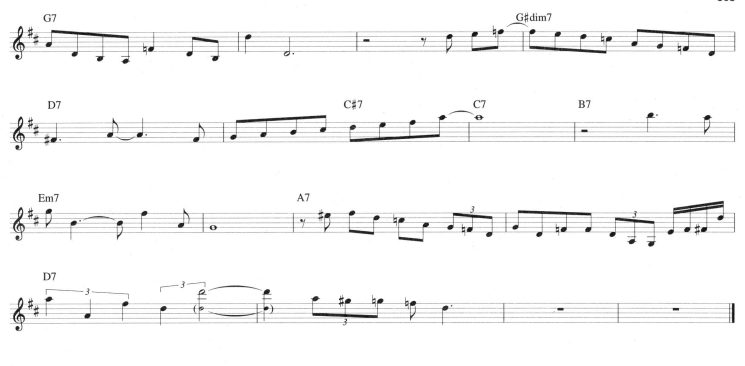

WEST COAST BLUES

By JOHN L. "WES" MONTGOMERY

TWO DEGREES EAST, THREE DEGREES WEST

By JOHN LEWIS

WHAT IS THERE TO SAY
from THE ZIEGFELD FOLLIES OF 1934

Words and Music by VERNON DUKE
and E.Y. HARBURG

WHEN SUNNY GETS BLUE

Lyric by JACK SEGAL
Music by MARVIN FISHER

WHAT DO YOU SEE

By ERNIE WATTS
and RIQUE PANTOJA

WHAT WILL I TELL MY HEART

Words and Music by IRVING GORDON,
PETE TINTURIN and JACK LAWRENCE

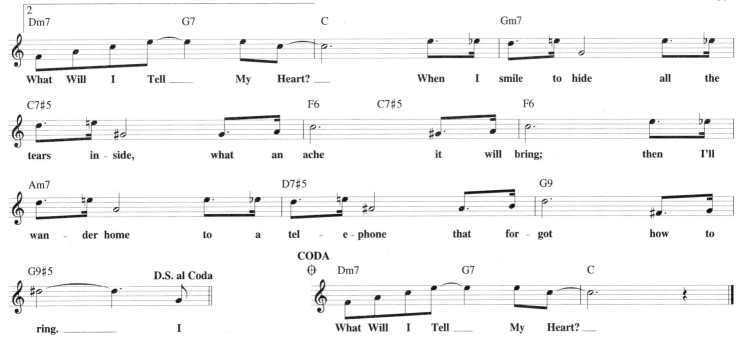

WHEN THE SUN COMES OUT

Lyric by TED KOEHLER
Music by HAROLD ARLEN

WHOLEY EARTH

Words and Music by
ABBEY LINCOLN

WHY WAS I BORN?
from SWEET ADELINE

Lyrics by OSCAR HAMMERSTEIN II
Music by JEROME KERN

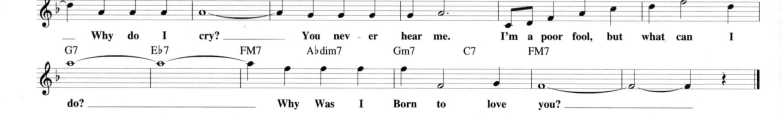

(There'll Be Blue Birds Over)
THE WHITE CLIFFS OF DOVER

Words by NAT BURTON
Music by WALTER KENT

Slowly

There'll be blue-birds o-ver The White Cliffs Of Do-ver to-mor-row, just you wait and see. _____ There'll be love and laugh-ter and peace e-ver af-ter, to-mor-row, when the world is free. _____ The shep-herd will tend his sheep, the val-ley will bloom a-gain. And Jim-my will go to sleep in his own lit-tle room a-gain. There'll be blue-birds o-ver The White Cliffs Of Do-ver to-mor-row, just you wait and see. _____ There'll be see.

1 F6 Gm7 C7
2 F6

WHY DON'T YOU DO RIGHT
(Get Me Some Money, Too!)

By JOE McCOY

Moderately

You had plen-ty mon-ey nine-teen twen-'y two, ___ you let oth-er peo-ple make a fool of you. _ Why Don't You Do Right, _____ like some oth-er men do? _____ Get out of here and get me some mon-ey too. _____ Yo' sit-tin' down won-d'ring what it's all a-bout, __ if you ain't got no mon-ey they will put you out. __ Why Don't You Do Right, _____ like some oth-er men do? _____ Get out of here and get me some mon-ey too. _____ If you had pre-pared __ twen-ty years a-go, ___ you would-n't be ___ wan-d'ring now from do' to do'. __ Why Don't You Do Right, ___ like some oth-er men do? _____ Get out of here and get me some mon-ey too.

WHAT'LL I DO?
from MUSIC BOX REVUE OF 1924

Words and Music by
IRVING BERLIN

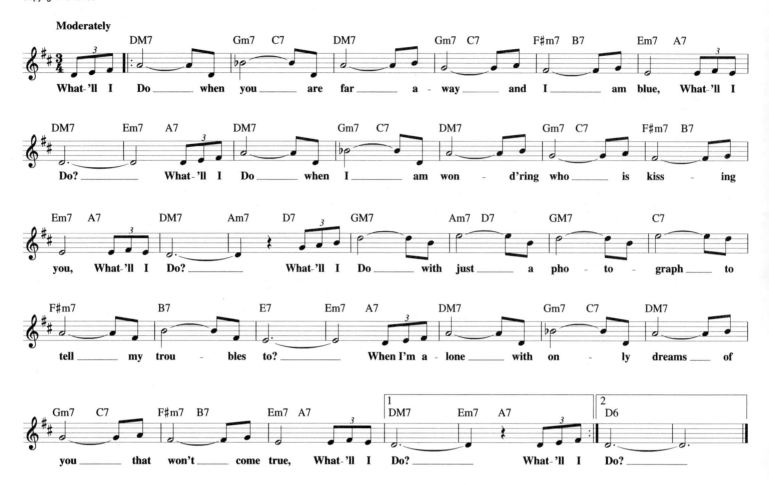

THE WIND

Music by RUSSELL FREEMAN
Lyrics by JERRY GLADSTONE

WINDOWS

By CHICK COREA

WINTERSONG

By PAUL DESMOND

WITHOUT A SONG

Words by WILLIAM ROSE and EDWARD ELISCU
Music by VINCENT YOUMANS

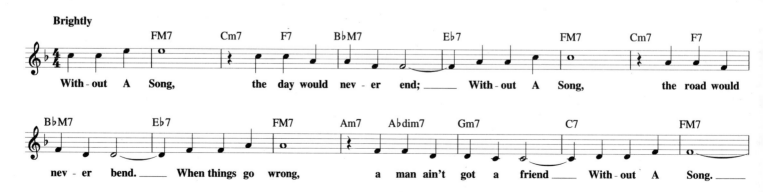

With-out A Song, the day would nev-er end; _____ With-out A Song, the road would

nev-er bend. _____ When things go wrong, a man ain't got a friend With-out A Song. _____

YOU'RE BLASÉ
from BOW BELLS

Words by BRUCE SIEVIER
Music by ORD HAMILTON

You're Everything

Lyric by NEVILLE POTTER
Music by CHICK COREA

WIVES AND LOVERS

(Hey, Little Girl)

from the Paramount Picture WIVES AND LOVERS

Words by HAL DAVID
Music by BURT BACHARACH

Moderately fast

Hey, lit - tle girl, comb your hair, fix your make - up, soon he will o - pen the door.
Day af - ter day there are girls at the of - fice and men will al - ways be men.

Don't think be - cause there's a ring on your fin - ger you need - n't try an - y - more. For
Don't send him off with your hair still in curl - ers, you may not see him a - gain, for

wives should al - ways be lov - ers too. Run to his arms the mo - ment
wives should al - ways be lov - ers too. Run to his arms the mo - ment

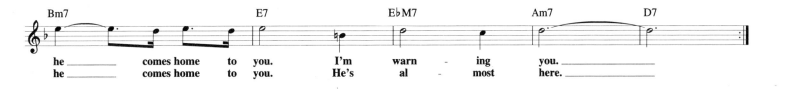

he comes home to you. I'm warn - ing you.
he comes home to you. He's al - most here.

Hey, lit - tle girl, bet - ter wear some - thing pret - ty, some - thing you'd wear to go to the cit - y. And

dim all the lights, pour the wine, start the mu - sic, time to get read - y for love. Oh,

time to get read - y, time to get read - y, time to get read - y for love.

WOODYN' YOU

By DIZZY GILLESPIE

YOU'RE NEARER
from TOO MANY GIRLS

Words by LORENZ HART
Music by RICHARD RODGERS

YOU'RE DRIVING ME CRAZY!
(What Did I Do?)

Words and Music by
WALTER DONALDSON

YOU'RE MINE YOU

Words by EDWARD HEYMAN
Music by JOHN W. GREEN

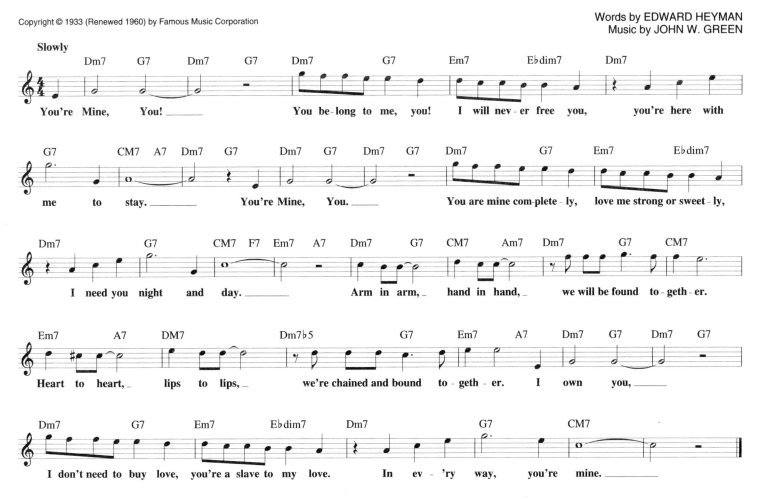

YOU ARE TOO BEAUTIFUL
from HALLELUJAH, I'M A BUM

Words by LORENZ HART
Music by RICHARD RODGERS

YOU COULDN'T BE CUTER
from JOY OF LIVING

Lyric by DOROTHY FIELDS
Music by JEROME KERN

You'll at tract all the rel-a-tives we have dodged for years and years. And what-'ll they tell me? Ex-act-ly what-'ll they tell me? They'll say you could-n't be nic-er, could-n't be sweet-er, could-n't be bet-ter, could-n't be smooth-er, could-n't be cut-er, ba-by, than you are! You are!

YOU BROUGHT A NEW KIND OF LOVE TO ME
from the Paramount Picture THE BIG POND

Words and Music by SAMMY FAIN,
IRVING KAHAL and PIERRE NORMAN

If the night-in-gales could sing like you, they'd sing much sweet-er than they do, for you've brought a new kind of love to me. If the sand-man brought me dreams of you, I'd want to sleep my whole life through, for you've brought a new kind of love to me. I know that I'm the slave, you're the queen, but still you can un-der-stand that un-der-neath it all, you're a maid and I am on-ly a man. I would work and slave the whole day through if I could hur-ry home to you, for you've brought a new kind of love to me.

YOU DON'T KNOW WHAT LOVE IS

Words and Music by DON RAYE
and GENE DePAUL

YOU'VE MADE ME SO VERY HAPPY

Words and Music by BERRY GORDY, FRANK E. WILSON,
BRENDA HOLLOWAY and PATRICE HOLLOWAY

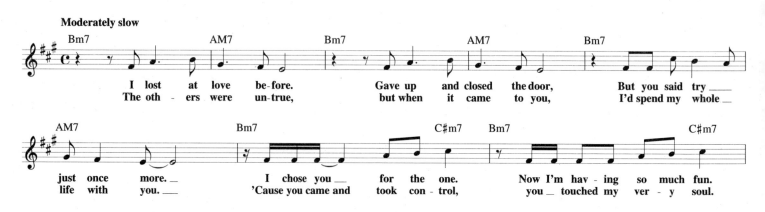

YOU LEAVE ME BREATHLESS
from the Paramount Motion Picture COCONUT GROVE

Words by RALPH FREED
Music by FREDERICK K. HOLLANDER

YOU TOOK ADVANTAGE OF ME
from PRESENT ARMS

Words by LORENZ HART
Music by RICHARD RODGERS

YOU'VE CHANGED

Words and Music by BILL CAREY
and CARL FISCHER

THE ULTIMATE JAZZ FAKE BOOK

FINALLY! THE JAZZ COLLECTION THAT EVERYONE'S BEEN WAITING FOR!

THE ULTIMATE JAZZ FAKE BOOK INCLUDES:

- More than 625 songs important to every jazz library.
- Carefully chosen chords with some common practice chord substitutions.
- Lyrics to accommodate vocalists.
- Easy-to-read music typography.
- Composer and performer indexes.

The selection of songs in *The Ultimate Jazz Fake Book* is a result of an exhaustive effort to represent the many styles of music that make up that beloved idiom we call jazz. The styles found in this collection include: traditional, swing, bebop, Latin/bossa nova, hard bop/modern jazz and Tin Pan Alley standards/show tunes.

MORE THAN 625 SONGS INCLUDING:

After You've Gone • Afternoon In Paris • Ain't Misbehavin' • Air Mail Special • All Of Me • All The Things You Are • Along Came Betty • Alright, Okay, You Win • Among My Souvenirs • And All That Jazz • Angel Eyes • Autumn Leaves • Baby, Won't You Please Come Home • Bag's Groove • Basin Street Blues • Bernie's Tune • Bewitched • Billie's Bounce • Birdland • Blue Champagne • Blues For Pablo • Bluesette • Body And Soul • Button Up Your Overcoat • Caldonia • Carolina Moon • C.C. Rider • Cherokee • Confirmation • Cry Me A River • Darn That Dream • Deed I Do • Dinah • Django • Do You Know What It Means To Miss New Orleans • Donna Lee • Don't Get Around Much Anymore • Donna Lee • Down By The Riverside • Ev'ry Time We Say Goodbye • Everybody Loves My Baby • Everything's Coming Up Roses • Falling In Love With Love • Fever • A Fine Romance • Fly Me To The Moon • A Foggy Day • (I Love You) For Sentimental Reasons • Four • Gee Baby, Ain't I Good To You • The Girl From Ipanema • The Glory Of Love • The Glow Worm • A Good Man Is Hard To Find • Groovin' High • Happy Talk • Harlem Nocturne • Haunted Heart • How High The Moon • I Can't Get Started • I Concentrate On You • I Could Write A Book • I Cover The Waterfront • I Don't Know Why (I Just Do) • I Got Plenty O' Nuttin' • I Love Paris • I Remember Duke • I'll Remember April • I'll Take Romance • I'm Old-Fashioned • If I Were A Bell • In A Little Spanish Town • In The Mood • Is You Is, Or Is You Ain't (Ma Baby) • It Might As Well Be Spring • It's Only A Paper Moon • Jelly Roll Blues • Jersey Bounce • The Joint Is Jumpin' • King Porter Stomp • The Lady Is A Tramp • Lester Left Town • Let's Call The Whole Thing Off • Let's Fall In Love • Little Boat • Little Brown Jug • Love For Sale • Love Walked In • Lullaby Of Birdland • Lush Life • Mad About The Boy • Malaguena • The Man That Got Away • Maple Leaf Rag • Misty • Moonglow • Moonlight In Vermont • More • Moten Swing • My Funny Valentine • My Melancholy Baby • My Romance • A Night In Tunisia • A Nightingale Sang In Berkeley Square • Old Devil Moon • One Note Samba • Opus One • Ornithology • Paper Doll • People Will Say We're In Love • Quiet Nights Of Quiet Stars • 'Round Midnight • Route 66 • Ruby, My Dear • Satin Doll • Sentimental Journey • Shivers • Skylark • Slightly Out Of Tune (Desafinado) • Solar • Solitude • Song For My Father • Speak Low • Stompin' At The Savoy • A String Of Pearls • Summer Samba • Take The "A" Train • There's A Small Hotel • The Thrill Is Gone • Tuxedo Junction • Undecided • Unforgettable • Waltz For Debby • 'Way Down Yonder In New Orleans • The Way You Look Tonight • We Kiss In A Shadow • When I Fall In Love • Witchcraft • Woodchopper's Ball • You Made Me Love You • You'd Be So Nice To Come Home To • You're My Everything • and many, many more!

Spanning more than nine decades of music, *The Ultimate Jazz Fake Book* fills a void for many musicians whose active repertories could not possibly include this vast collection of classic jazz compositions and durable songs.